Christ's Mission Through the Church
A Primary Source Reader

Robert J. Brancatelli

saint mary's press

The publishing team included Gloria Shahin, editorial director; and Joanna Dailey, development editor. Prepress and manufacturing coordinated by the production departments of Saint Mary's Press.

Cover Image: © The Crosiers / Gene Plaisted, OSC

Printed in the United States of America

1361

ISBN 978-1-59982-139-9, print

Contents

Introduction

Welcome to this collection of primary source readings presented here to enhance your study of the Church. This text is meant to broaden your understanding of the Church so that you can see what the Church means for you personally, for other Christians, and for the wider society.

In it you will find an eclectic and fascinating collection of essays from all kinds of people, from Popes, bishops, priests, and martyrs to an evolutionary biologist, two novelists, a young Jewish woman, and a pioneer in the cause of social justice for the poor. They write about all kinds of wonderful things, including the rich history of the Church, her great witnesses, and the struggles that all of us go through to live our faith meaningfully and allow it to come alive in our everyday lives.

There are many themes throughout these chapters. You will discover writings about the Body of Christ; the meaning of mystery at the core not just of faith but of personhood; suffering and persecution as they relate to discipleship; and the relation between science and our belief in things that transcend the physical.

Perhaps the most important theme, however, one that is not explicit but weaves its way quietly through these chapters, is that we're all in this together. No matter who we are, where we come from, or how we got here, we have been called to be part of the people of God. God stands with us in community in good times and bad, whether we have been blessed with long life and material success or have suffered great pain and loss.

Being in this together means that we need not fear anything. This is a powerful claim but one that is easy to forget, which is why Saint Paul reminds us: "For I am convinced that neither death, nor life, nor angels, nor principalities, nor present things nor future things, nor powers, nor height, nor depth, nor any other creature will be able to separate us from the love of God in Christ Jesus our Lord" (Romans 8:38–39).

As you read the chapters that follow, keep this in mind. Make it your daily prayer as we, together, follow Jesus as his disciples, his brothers and sisters, his beloved community, the Church.

Part 1
Christ Established His One Church to Continue His Presence and His Work

1 The Church Proclaims Jesus Christ

Introduction

The excerpt you are about to read from the Acts of the Apostles may be quite familiar to you already. You may have come across it in previous studies, at a retreat, or in preparation for Confirmation. Part of it is proclaimed in the Liturgy of the Word during the Easter season. If you are a lector in your parish, chances are you have proclaimed what is arguably the most difficult tongue-twister in the entire lectionary. Chapter 2, verses 9 through 11, includes a listing of travelers to Jerusalem for the celebration of Pentecost: "We are Parthians, Medes, and Elamites, inhabitants of Mesopotamia, Judea and Cappadocia, Pontus and Asia, Phrygia and Pamphylia, Egypt and the districts of Libya near Cyrene, as well as travelers from Rome."

> **Pentecost**
>
> The word *pentecost* is Greek for "fiftieth day." For Jews it was a celebration of the first fruits of the harvest and a commemoration of the Law of Moses. It was celebrated fifty days after Passover. For Christians Pentecost celebrates the descent of the Holy Spirit fifty days after the Resurrection of Christ. In the Catholic Church, this feast is given the highest rank, that of a *solemnity*.

But beyond the difficulty of proclamation, chapter 2 of Acts gives us an inside view of the Church in the first century. Specifically, it tells us what was considered necessary to be a disciple of Jesus, the preacher who was crucified by the Romans but then was resurrected by the "right hand of God" (v. 33). For instance, in verses 38 and 39, Peter tells those gathered that they must turn back to God and have their sins forgiven through Baptism. They will receive the gift of the Holy Spirit. Then he adds something quite extraordinary: Jesus' message of salvation is not just for those assembled but for everyone: "For the promise is made to you and to your children and to all those far off, whomever the Lord our God will call" (Acts of the Apostles 2:39). Although he was referring to Jews throughout the Mediterranean, eventually the Church and her message of salvation—called the *kerygma*—spread beyond Judea to Samaria, the Middle East, and the rest of the Roman Empire (see Ephesians 3:4–6).

Chapter 2 also describes a fourfold pattern of Christian living. In verses 42 through 47, we see that the community of believers "devoted themselves to the teaching of the apostles," (v. 42) helped one another by sharing possessions and property, broke bread together (what we now know as the Eucharist), and praised God in prayer. They were united and nourished by the Holy Spirit, which descended upon them and gave them new life. This is the central theme of the Acts of the Apostles, which continues the story begun in the Gospel of Luke by proclaiming that the promise of salvation has been given to everyone in Christ's name through the Holy Spirit. As you read this selection, try to identify some basic elements of Christian life and teaching that can still be found in the Church today.

> *kerygma* Greek for "proclamation." Refers to the preaching of the Word of God as Gospel, or the Good News of salvation, offered to all through Jesus Christ. *Kerygma* has two senses. It is both an event of proclamation and a message proclaimed. See Romans 10:14 and Acts 8:31; for the "Easter *kerygma*," see 1 Corinthians 15:3–5.

Excerpt from the Acts of the Apostles, Chapter 2

When the time for Pentecost was fulfilled, they were all in one place together. And suddenly there came from the sky a noise like a strong driving wind, and it filled the entire house in which they were. Then there appeared to them tongues as of fire, which parted and came to rest on each one of them. And they were all filled with the holy Spirit and began to speak in different tongues, as the Spirit enabled them to proclaim.

Now there were devout Jews from every nation under heaven staying in Jerusalem. At this sound, they gathered in a large crowd, but they were confused because each one heard them speaking in his own language. They were astounded, and in amazement they asked, "Are not all these people who are speaking Galileans? Then how does each of us hear them in his own native language? We are Parthians, Medes, and Elamites, inhabitants of Mesopotamia, Judea and Cappadocia, Pontus and Asia, Phrygia and Pamphylia, Egypt and the districts of Libya near Cyrene, as well as travelers from Rome, both Jews and converts to Judaism, Cretans and Arabs, yet we hear them speaking in our own tongues of the mighty acts of God." They were all astounded and bewildered, and said to one another, "What does this mean?" But others said, scoffing, "They have had too much new wine."

Then Peter stood up with the Eleven, raised his voice, and proclaimed to them, "You who are Jews, indeed all of you staying in Jerusalem. Let this be known to you, and listen to my words. These people are not drunk, as you suppose, for it is only nine o'clock in the morning. No, this is what was spoken through the prophet Joel:

'It will come to pass in the last days,' God says,
    'that I will pour out a portion of my spirit upon all flesh.
Your sons and your daughters shall prophesy,
    your young men shall see visions,
    your old men shall dream dreams.
Indeed, upon my servants and my handmaids
    I will pour out a portion of my spirit in those days,
    and they shall prophesy.
And I will work wonders in the heavens above
    and signs on the earth below:
    blood, fire, and a cloud of smoke.
The sun shall be turned to darkness,
    and the moon to blood,
    before the coming of the great and splendid day of the Lord,
and it shall be that everyone shall be saved
    who calls on the name of the Lord.'

You who are Israelites, hear these words. Jesus the Nazorean was a man commended to you by God with mighty deeds, wonders, and signs, which

God worked through him in your midst, as you yourselves know. This man, delivered up by the set plan and foreknowledge of God, you killed, using lawless men to crucify him. But God raised him up, releasing him from the throes of death, because it was impossible for him to be held by it. For David says of him:

> 'I saw the Lord ever before me,
>> with him at my right hand I shall not be disturbed.
> Therefore my heart has been glad and my tongue has exulted;
>> my flesh, too, will dwell in hope,
> because you will not abandon my soul to the netherworld,
>> nor will you suffer your holy one to see corruption.
> You have made known to me the paths of life;
>> you will fill me with joy in your presence.'

My brothers, one can confidently say to you about the patriarch David that he died and was buried, and his tomb is in our midst to this day. But since he was a prophet and knew that God had sworn an oath to him that he would set one of his descendants upon his throne, he foresaw and spoke of the resurrection of the Messiah, that neither was he abandoned to the netherworld nor did his flesh see corruption. God raised this Jesus; of this we are all witnesses. Exalted at the right hand of God, he received the promise of the holy Spirit from the Father and poured it forth, as you (both) see and hear. For David did not go up into heaven, but he himself said:

> 'The Lord said to my Lord, "Sit at my right hand
>> until I make your enemies your footstool."'

Therefore let the whole house of Israel know for certain that God has made him both Lord and Messiah, this Jesus whom you crucified."

Now when they heard this, they were cut to the heart, and they asked Peter and the other apostles, "What are we to do, my brothers?" Peter [said] to them, "Repent and be baptized, every one of you, in the name of Jesus Christ for the forgiveness of your sins; and you will receive the gift of the holy Spirit. For the promise is made to

> 66 **God has made him both Lord and Messiah, this Jesus whom you crucified.** 99

you and to your children and to all those far off, whomever the Lord our God will call." He testified with many other arguments, and was exhorting them, "Save yourselves from this corrupt generation." Those who accepted his message were baptized, and about three thousand persons were added that day.

They devoted themselves to the teaching of the apostles and to the communal life, to the breaking of the bread and to the prayers. Awe came upon everyone, and many wonders and signs were done through the apostles. All who believed were together and had all things in common; they would sell their property and possessions and divide them among all according to each one's need. Every day they devoted themselves to meeting together in the temple area and to breaking bread in their homes. They ate their meals with exultation and sincerity of heart, praising God and enjoying favor with all the people. And every day the Lord added to their number those who were being saved.

For Reflection

1. In his speech to the crowd, Saint Peter states the need for repentance. Why is this so important, and where do you see the need for repentance in your life?

2. Why does Peter state emphatically that "God raised this Jesus; of this we are all witnesses" (2:32)?

3. What do you think of the members of the early Church sharing their possessions with others, "according to each one's need" (2:45)? Would you be willing to do that?

2 Witness to Christ

Introduction

Saint Ignatius was Bishop of Antioch in Syria. He lived during the time of the Roman emperor Trajan (98–107 BC) and was martyred in the Flavian Amphitheatre (the Coliseum) in Rome around 107 BC. This chapter's reading (from the *Epistle of Saint Ignatius to the Romans*) is taken from his letter to the Christians of Rome, which he wrote while under military escort from Smyrna, in Turkey, to Rome for his trial. At the time, Christianity had been outlawed, and Christians were required to worship the emperor as a god, which Ignatius and many others refused to do. He is explicit in this letter about what will become of him in Rome but knows that "Jesus Christ will give me my liberty, and in Him I shall rise again as a free man." To understand the circumstances in which this letter was written, it is necessary to understand martyrdom.

Martyrdom was a harsh but commonplace reality in the life of the early Church. We have numerous accounts of Christians who were put to death because of their faith, such as Saints Stephen, Peter, Paul, Ignatius, Polycarp, Perpetua, and Felicity. Roman authorities viewed Christians as a threat to the social and political stability of the empire, and thus they were executed in dramatic fashion. The Roman historian Tacitus even refers to Christianity as "a deadly superstition," both "sleaze-ridden and shameful." Part of the revulsion Romans may have felt toward Christianity was the belief that Christians ate flesh and were cannibalistic, which is a misconception that Ignatius turns to great rhetorical advantage in referring to his own body in Eucharistic images (e.g., "I am His wheat, ground fine by the lions' teeth to be made purest bread for Christ").

Martyrdom is also characteristic of the Church in modern times in places like South and Central America, Eastern Europe, Africa, and Asia, where many—from ordinary Christians to catechists and bishops—have been killed and many continue to die for their faith. It seems, then, that giving witness to the faith is not an "extra" or an adornment but rather part and parcel of what it means to be a Christian.

In his *Epistle to the Romans*, Ignatius identifies his experience of imprisonment and impending death with the Crucifixion of Christ. Ignatius sees the suffering to come as his way to full life in Jesus Christ, and so begs his friends in Rome not to intercede for his release. His writing is replete with Eucharistic images, as he compares himself to the Eucharistic bread that is broken so that the life of Christ may abound. Ignatius cautions Christians not to be hypocrites, claiming one thing but acting in an entirely different manner. He was, perhaps, ahead of his time in exhorting his readers to get real: "Do not have Jesus Christ on your lips, and the world in your heart." In a significant way, this letter is "the last will and testament" of a martyr and a saint and gives an important witness to the faith of the early Church.

Excerpt from *The Epistle to the Romans*
By Saint Ignatius of Antioch

4. For my part, I am writing to all the churches and assuring them that I am truly in earnest about dying for God—if only you yourselves put no obstacles in the way. I must implore you to do me no such untimely kindness; pray leave me to be a meal for the beasts, for it is they who can provide my way to God. I am His wheat, ground fine by the lions' teeth to be made purest bread[1] for Christ. Better still, incite the creatures to become a sepulchre for me; let them not leave the smallest scrap of my flesh, so that I need not be a burden to anyone after I fall asleep. When there is no trace of my body left for the world to see, then I shall truly be Jesus Christ's disciple. So intercede with Him for me, that by their instru-

mentality I may be made a sacrifice to God. However, I am not issuing orders to you, as though I were a Peter or a Paul.[2] They were Apostles, and I am a condemned criminal. They were free men, and I am still a slave[3] (though if I suffer, Jesus Christ will give me my liberty, and in Him I shall rise again as a free man). For the present, these chains are schooling me to have done with earthly desires.

5. All the same, I have already been finding myself in conflict with beasts of prey by land and by sea,[4] by night and by day, the whole way from Syria to Rome; chained as I am to a half-a-score of savage leopards[5] (in other words, a detachment of soldiers), who only grow more insolent the more gratuities they are given. Still, their ill-usage does at least enable me to make some progress in discipleship; though that is not to say that my sins are yet wholly absolved. How I look forward to the real lions that have been got ready for me! All I pray is that I may find them swift. I am going to make overtures to them, so that, unlike some other wretches whom they have been too spiritless to touch, they may devour me with all speed. And if they are still reluctant, I shall use force to them. You must forgive me, but I do know what is best for myself. This is the first stage of my discipleship; and no power, visible or invisible, must grudge me my coming to Jesus Christ. Fire, cross, beast-fighting, hacking and quartering, splintering of bone and mangling of limb, even the pulverizing of my entire body—let every horrid and diabolical torment come upon me, provided only that I can win my way to Jesus Christ!

Persecutions

Because Christianity was not afforded the benefits of protected religions in the Roman Empire (as Judaism was, for example), Christians were singled out for persecution simply because of their faith. The first major persecution occurred during Nero's reign (AD 64), with another during the reign of Domitian (AD 95), and continuing through Decius (AD 250) and Galerius in the east (AD 311). Emperor Constantine, a convert to Christianity, later granted toleration to Christianity, which became the state religion through the Edict of Thessalonica (AD 380).

6. All the ends of the earth, all the kingdoms of the world would be of no profit to me; so far as I am concerned, to die in Jesus Christ is better than to be monarch of earth's widest bounds. He who died for us is all that I seek; He who rose again for us is my whole desire. The pangs of birth are upon me; have patience with me, my brothers, and do not shut me out from life, do not wish me to be stillborn. Here is one who only longs to be God's; do not make a present of him to the world again, or delude him with the things of earth. Suffer me to attain to light, light pure and undefiled; for only when I am come thither shall I be truly a man. Leave me to imitate the Passion of my God. If any of you has God within himself, let that man understand my longings, and feel for me, because he will know the forces by which I am constrained.

7. It is the hope of this world's prince to get hold of me and undermine my resolve, set as it is upon God. Pray let none of you lend him any assistance, but take my part instead, for it is the part of God. Do not have Jesus Christ on your lips, and the world in your heart; do not cherish thoughts of grudging me my fate. Even if I were to come and implore you in person, do not yield to my pleading; keep your compliance for this written entreaty instead. Here and now, as I write in the fullness of life, I am yearning for death with all the passion of a lover. Earthly longings have been crucified; in me there is left no spark of desire for mundane things, but only a murmur of living water that whispers within me, 'Come to the Father.' There is no pleasure for me in any meats that perish, or in the delights of this life; I am **fain** for the bread of God, even the flesh of Jesus Christ, who is the seed of David; and for my drink I crave that Blood of His which is love imperishable.

8. I want no more of what men call life. And my want can come true, if it is your desire. Pray, then, let it be your desire; so that in your turn you also may be desired.[6] Not to write at more length, I appeal to you to believe me. Jesus Christ will make it clear to you that I am speaking the truth; he is a faithful mouthpiece, by which the Father's words of truth find utterance. Intercede for me, then, that I may have my wish; for I am not writing now as a mere man, but I am voicing the

fain Archaic, meaning "desirous of."

mind of God. My suffering will be a proof of your goodwill; my rejection, a proof of your disfavour.

9. Remember the church of Syria in your prayers; it has God for its pastor now, in place of myself, and Jesus Christ alone will have the oversight of it—He, and your own love. As for me, I feel shame to be styled one of its members; I have no right at all to the name, for I was the very last of them all, an embryo born untimely[7] (though if I ever manage to reach the presence of God, by His mercy I shall be somebody then).

> 66 *In me there is left no spark of desire for mundane things, but only a murmur of living water that whispers within me, 'Come to the Father.'* 99

I greet you in spirit; and the churches who have been my hosts in the name of Jesus Christ also send you their love. (It was no common wayfarer's welcome I have had from them, for even churches that were not naturally on my route at all came and escorted me from one city to the next.)

10. This letter comes to you from Smyrna, by the hands of our praiseworthy men of Ephesus. Crocus, specially dear to me, is here too, and a number of others besides. I believe you have already been told of certain persons who went on ahead of me from Syria to Rome, for the glory of God. Tell them that I am not far away now. One and all, they have deserved well of God and of you; and it is only right for you to do what you can to set their minds at rest.

As I write this, it is the twenty-fourth of August. Farewell now until the end, and wait with patience for Jesus Christ.

Endnotes

1. Only bread of the finest quality, as a symbol of purity, was used in sacrificial offerings.
2. Both of whom had been at Rome, and spoken with apostolic authority to the Roman church.
3. This has led some commentators to think that Ignatius had been, or perhaps still was, an actual slave. It may only refer, however, to his present helpless condition.
4. If this is meant literally, we must assume that the first stage of his journey had been made by ship from Seleucia (the port of Antioch) to Attalia, in Pamphylia. From there the party could make their way overland to Laodicea.
5. This is the earliest known occurrence of the word in literature. Since leopards were well known in Syria (whence they were sometimes brought for exhibition at Rome) the comparison would come naturally to Ignatius.
6. i.e., by God.
7. St Paul, too, describes himself in the same way (1 Cor. xv, 8). Here, as there, the image suggests both a sudden conversion to Christianity, and a slow and feeble growth.

For Reflection

1. What does Ignatius mean when he says: "You must forgive me, but I do know what is best for myself. This is the first stage of my discipleship; and no power, visible or invisible, must grudge me my coming to Jesus Christ"?

2. Scholars believe that Ignatius is writing to the Church of Rome so that it will not intercede on his behalf and, possibly, have his life spared. Why do you think Ignatius would ask this of his Christian friends?

3. What can we learn about the Eucharist from Ignatius's many references to and love for the Body and Blood of Christ?

3 The Church Expands

Introduction

Augustine, saint and Doctor of the Church, was born in the ancient city of Thagaste in North Africa (modern Algeria) in AD 354. The chronicle of his conversion to Christianity in his *Confessions* has been a staple of Christian spirituality and moral formation for centuries. In it Augustine tells of his dissolute life and sexual promiscuity as a young man, his conversion experience in Milan, Italy, in July 386, and his baptism by Saint Ambrose, Bishop of Milan, the following Easter.

> **Doctor of the Church**
>
> The Church gives this title to men and women who have contributed to the Church's learning and spirituality through their scholarship and saintliness. Four of the early Church Fathers have been named Doctors of the Church: Pope Saint Gregory the Great, Saint Ambrose (Bishop of Milan), Saint Augustine of Hippo, and Saint Jerome, who translated the Bible from its original languages into Latin.

Following his conversion and baptism, Augustine returned to North Africa and devoted himself to a life of prayer, fasting, and study. He later became a priest and then Bishop of Hippo in 395. His writings have become classics in the Christian canon, particularly such works as *On the Trinity* (*De Trinitate*) and *The City of God* (*De Civitate Dei*).

In *The City of God,* from which you will read an excerpt in this chapter, Augustine sets out for the reader two ways of being human: an earthly way filled with selfishness, jealousy, corruption, and sin, and a heavenly way characterized by trust in God and selfless love of both God and neighbor. Writing in a time when the Roman Empire was facing an onslaught of invasions and was

> ### The City of God
>
> Saint Augustine wrote *The City of God* in AD 413 to 427. It is considered to be his masterpiece. In this book Augustine lays out a plan for the Church to be a beacon of hope for the world and instructs individual Christians to be "in the world but not of it," that is, doing good in society but not influenced by society's harmful choices (see John 17:15–16, in which Jesus prays that his followers in the world be kept from evil).

becoming increasingly weakened, Augustine was defending the Christian faith from those who accused it of causing the breakdown and weakening of the empire. He was also describing the distinctly Christian lifestyle—one which he himself followed—of charity, prudence, and moral courage in the face not only of the invasions but of persecutions and challenges to orthodox Christian teaching. Augustine viewed the world as corrupt but the City of God as a place where justice reigned and the love of God pervaded all hearts so that suffering was no more and the city was filled with the natural light of Christ. He recognized, however, not only that the two cities were distinct but also that the City of God would be realized only in the next life.

In this selection from *The City of God,* Augustine describes the Church's expansion beyond Judea and Samaria, highlighting the role of persecution. He exhorts his readers to stand firm until the end, for they will be justified in their faith and resurrected by Christ. Quoting Saint Paul, he reminds us that "all those who want to live piously in Christ Jesus will suffer persecution." Augustine died in AD 430, as Hippo was facing the threat of a **Vandal** invasion. Augustine's writings assured the Christians of his time, and ours, that the Church would endure, even through times of persecution and civil destruction.

Vandals A Germanic tribe that sacked Rome in 455. *Vandalism* has come to mean senseless destruction.

Excerpt from *The City of God*

By Saint Augustine of Hippo

CHAPTER 50

The Church expanded from Jerusalem out, in accordance with the well-known prophecy: 'The Lord's commands shall go out from Sion, his word from Jerusalem,' (Isa. 2.3) and with what our Lord said to His disciples who were marveling over His Resurrection from the dead: 'He opened their minds that they might understand the Scriptures, and said to them: Thus is it written; and thus the Christ should suffer, and should rise again from the dead on the third day; and that repentance and remission of sins should be preached in his name to all the nations, beginning from Jerusalem.' (Luke 24.45–47) This prediction was repeated when He answered their question about His second coming by saying: 'It is not for you to know the times or dates which the Father has fixed by his own authority; but you shall receive power when the Holy Spirit comes upon you, and you shall be witnesses for me in Jerusalem, and in all Judea and Samaria and even to the very ends of the earth.' (Acts 1.7,8)

It was only after many in Judea and Samaria had believed that the disciples went out to other peoples to preach the Gospel, like lamps which the Lord had equipped with the wick of His word and lit with the light of the Holy Spirit. For He had told them: 'Do not be afraid of those who kill the body but cannot kill the soul.' But they were so hotly fired with love that they did not feel this chilling fear. In this spirit the Gospel was preached throughout the whole world—to the accompaniment of horrendous persecutions, manifold torturings, and death of martyrs—by men who had seen and heard Christ before His passion and after His resurrection and by those who carried on where they left off. Meanwhile, God gave them solemn attestation by signs and wonders and various **prodigies**; and by the gifts of the Holy Spirit, too.

As a result, the Gentiles believed in Him who had died for their redemption

> **prodigies** Unusual, extraordinary, or inexplicable accomplishments, deeds, or events.

and began, with Christian tenderness, to venerate the martyrs' blood—the very blood they had spilled in diabolical fury. Even the kings whose laws had depopulated the Church came to bow down before that saving Name, which their earlier savagery had tried to abolish from the earth, and even undertook to drive out the false gods for whose sake they had persecuted the worshipers of the true God.

CHAPTER 51

When the Devil saw the human race abandoning the temples of demons and marching happily forward in the name of the freedom-giving Mediator, he inspired heretics to oppose Christian teaching under cover of the Christian name as though their presence in the City of God could go unchallenged like the presence, in the city of confusion, of philosophers with wholly different and even contradictory opinions!

Heretics are those who entertain in Christ's Church unsound and distorted ideas and stubbornly refuse, even when warned, to return to what is sound and right, to correct their contagious and death-dealing doctrines, but go on defending them. When they leave the Church they are ranked as enemies who try her patience. Even so, their evil-doing profits the loyal Catholic members of Christ's Body, for God makes good use of bad men, 'while for those who love God all things work together unto good.' (Rom. 8.28) Actually, all foes of the Church, whether blinded by error or moved by malice, subserve her in some fashion. If they have power to do her physical harm, they develop her power to suffer; if they oppose her intellectually, they bring out her Wisdom; since she must love even her enemies her loving kindness is made manifest; and whether she has to deal with them in the persuasiveness of argument or the chastisement of law, they bring into play her power to do good.

So it is that the diabolical prince of the ungodly city is not allowed to harm the pilgrim City of God, even when he stirs up his tools and dupes against her. Beyond all doubt, **Divine Providence** sees to it that she has both some solace of prosperity that she may not be broken

Divine Providence The guidance, material goods, and care provided by God that is sufficient to meet our needs.

by adversity and some testing of adversity that she may not be weakened by prosperity. Thus, the one balances the other, as one can see from the words of the psalm, 'According to the multitude of sorrows in my heart, so thy consolations have gladdened my soul,' (Ps. 93.19) and those of St. Paul: 'Rejoicing in hope, being patient in tribulation.' (Rom. 12.12)

St. Paul also says: 'All who want to live piously in Christ Jesus will suffer persecution.' (2 Tim. 3.12) Persecution, therefore, will never be lacking. For, when our enemies from without leave off raging and there ensues a span of tranquility—even of genuine tranquility and great consolation at least to the weak—we are not without enemies within, the many whose scandalous lives wound the hearts of the devout. These people bring discredit upon the Christian and Catholic name—a name so dear to 'all who want to live piously in Christ Jesus'—that they grieve bitterly to see their own brethren love it less than pious people should. There is that other heartache of seeing heretics, too, using the name and sacraments, the Scriptures and the Creed of genuine Christians. They realize how many would-be converts are driven into perplexed hesitancy because of heretical dissension, while the foul-mouthed find in heretics further pretext for cursing the Christian name, since these heretics at least call themselves Christian.

So it is that those who want to live piously in Christ must suffer the spiritual persecution of these and other aberrations in thought and morals, even when they are free from physical violence and vexation. This explains the verse: 'According to the multitude of sorrows in my heart'—there is no mention of the body. On the other hand, they recall the unchangeable, divine promise that no one of them can be lost. As St. Paul says: 'The Lord knows who are his,' (2 Tim. 2.19) and 'For those whom he has foreknown he has also predestined to become conformed to the image of his son.' (Rom. 8.29) And the psalm just cited goes on: 'Thy consolations have gladdened my soul.'

Yet, even the mental suffering which the devout undergo because of the lives of bad or pretended Christians is a source of spiritual profit because it flows from their charity, in virtue of which they would not have sinners be lost or go on blocking the salvation of others. Besides, the

> 66 *So it falls out that in this world, . . . the Church walks onward like a wayfarer stricken by the world's hostility, but comforted by the mercy of God.* 99

devout experience immense consolation when conversions flood the souls with a joy as great as the previous anguish on their account was excruciating.

So it falls out that in this world, in evil days like these, the Church walks onward like a wayfarer stricken by the world's hostility, but comforted by the mercy of God. Nor does this state of affairs date only from the days of Christ's and His Apostles' presence on earth. It was never any different from the days when the first just man, Abel, was slain by his ungodly brother. So it shall be until this world is no more.

For Reflection

1. Dividing human existence into two realms is a form of dualism, which is "either / or" thinking. Do you agree with Augustine's dualistic logic and his assessment of earthly life as sinful and corrupt? Explain.

2. Augustine mentions "Divine Providence," or God acting in the lives of individual believers, as well as in the entire Church. Do you believe that all things happen according to providence, that is, for a reason? Explain your answer.

3. Augustine explains that, in the life of the Church, adversity is balanced with prosperity. How do you see the Church experiencing both adversity and prosperity today?

4 The Body of the Church

Introduction

Mystery is a word that you will find throughout this book, because it is used by many of the writers whose works are included here to describe not only their personal journeys of faith but also the nature and purpose of the Church. You will even encounter the term used as an image of the Church. If it seems like an odd word to describe the Church, then we must find out what these authors mean by it and how their understanding differs from the common one.

In common usage today, *mystery* refers to a problem or dilemma that can be solved by applying the right kind of information. To us, a mystery is like a jigsaw puzzle that requires us to figure out how to put the pieces together and, after a while, the picture becomes clearer and it is just a matter of time before the puzzle is solved.

Yet *mystery* as a way to describe the Church is different. Saint Peter Damian, the writer of this chapter's excerpt, certainly understood it differently. For him, an eleventh-century bishop of Ostia, in Italy, the Church was a living body composed of many members: arms, ears, tongue, mouth, nostrils, feet, and so on, each with a specific purpose. This was not a new idea, for Saint Paul had described the Church as a body made up of different members, each fulfilling a certain function, like teacher or prophet, and bestowing certain gifts (see 1 Corinthians 12:4–31 in "The Church as Body" in part 2 of this book). To this basic understanding of the Church as the Body of Christ, Peter Damian added a subtle distinction.

As we will discover in the following reading, Peter Damian explained that the mystery of the Church as body is not so much that it has parts but rather that the whole is represented in each part and each part constitutes the whole. This mystery of "inward unity" is brought about by the Holy Spirit, who is "both one and manifold," just as all parts of the Church "form a single whole" yet are manifold. The mystery is that this singleness and multiplicity exist in the body of the Church *at the same time*. Thus, for Peter Damian, mystery was not a problem to be solved but the opposite: a paradox of life in which things do not make sense in the usual way but are filled with God's grace so that the closer we get to them, the less we really know and the more we need to rely on God.

According to Peter Damian, the paradox of the mystery of the Church is this: the Church is both one in many and many in one. The Church is made up of many Christians, and each single Christian embodies the entire Church.

Excerpt from *The Book of the Lord Be with You*
By Saint Peter Damian

CHAPTER FIVE

Indeed, the Church of Christ is united in all her parts by such a bond of love that her several members form a single body and in each one the whole Church is mystically present; so that the whole Church universal may rightly be called the one bride of Christ, and on the other hand every single soul can, because of the mystical effect of the sacrament, be regarded as the whole Church. Certainly Isaac with his prophetic nostrils could detect the presence of the whole Church when he said concerning one of his sons: 'See, the smell of my son is as the smell of a field.' (Gen. xxvii, 27) And that widow who was in debt and who at Elisha's command scattered her too small quantity of oil like seed and soon reaped a rich harvest when it overflowed her vessels was undoubtedly a symbol of the Church.

If we look carefully through the fields of the Holy Scriptures we will find that one man or one woman often represents the Church. For though because of the multitude of her peoples the Church seems to be of many parts, yet she is nevertheless one and simple in the mystical unity of one faith and one divine baptism. And although the seven women had a single husband, (Isa. iv, 1) a single virgin was said to be espoused to the heavenly bridegroom. Of her the apostle says: 'I have espoused you to one husband, that I may present you as a chaste virgin to Christ.' (2 Cor. xi, 2)

Now it can be clearly deduced from all this, as I said before that since the whole Church is represented in the person of one man, and because of this is called a single virgin, holy Church is one in all her

> **Scriptural Allusions**
>
> Theologians such as Peter Damian write for an audience that knows Scripture well, and thus they use Scripture to illustrate their points. In this excerpt, "the Apostle" refers to Saint Paul and his letters to the early Church. "Isaac and Jacob" refers to Isaac's blessing of his son, Jacob, in Genesis 27:27–29. The reference to Elisha and the widow refers to 2 Kings 4:1–7, in which the miracle of Elisha the prophet saves a woman's children from slavery.

members, and complete in each of them; her many members form a single whole in the unity of faith, and her many parts are united in each member by the bond of charity and the various gifts of grace, since all of these proceed from one source.

CHAPTER SIX

For indeed, although holy Church is divided in the multiplicity of her members, yet she is fused into unity by the fire of the Holy Spirit; and so even if she seems, as far as her situation in the world is concerned, to be scattered, yet the mystery of her inward unity can never be marred in its integrity. 'The love of God is shed abroad in our hearts by the Holy Ghost which is given unto us.' (Rom. v, 5) This Spirit is indeed without doubt both one and manifold; one in the essence of His greatness, and manifold in the diverse gifts of His grace, and He gives to holy Church, which He fills, this power: that all her parts shall form a single whole, and that each part shall contain the whole. This mystery of undivided unity was asked for by Truth Himself when He said to His Father concerning His disciples: 'I do not pray for these alone, but for them also who shall believe in Me through their word; that they may all be one; as Thou, Father, art in Me and I in Thee, that they also may be one in us: that the world may believe that Thou hast sent Me. And the glory which Thou gavest Me I have given them; that they may be one, even as we are one.' (John xvii, 20–22)

If, therefore, those who believe in Christ are one, then wherever we find a member according to outward appearances, there, by the mystery of the sacrament, the whole body is present. And so whatever belongs to the whole applies in some measure to the part; so that there is no absurdity in one man saying by himself anything which the body of the Church as a whole may utter, and in the same way many may fittingly give voice to that which is properly said by one person. Hence, when we are all assembled together we can rightly say: 'Bow down thine ear O Lord and hear me: for I am poor and needy. Preserve my soul, for I am holy.' (Ps. lxxxvi, 1–2) And when we are by ourselves, there is no incongruity in our singing: 'Sing aloud unto God our strength: make a joyful noise unto the God of Jacob.' (Ps. lxxxi, 1) And it is not irrelevant that many of us say together: 'I will bless the Lord at all times: his praise shall continually be in my mouth'; (Ps. xxxiv, 1) or that often when we are alone we sing with many tongues: 'O magnify the Lord with me, and let us exalt his name together' (Ps. xxxiv, 1) and other things of this kind. For on the One hand the solitariness of a single person does no harm to the words of many; and on the other the vast number of the faithful does not prejudice their unity since by the power of the Holy Spirit who is in each of us and fills the whole our solitude is manifold and our multiplicity singular.

> " And so it is clear that any action of an individual member is the work of the whole body; and conversely each of the parts participates in the action of the body as a whole. "

CHAPTER NINE

Moreover the eyes, tongue, feet and hands each have their own particular function in the human body; yet the hands do not touch, the feet do not walk, the tongue does not speak nor the eyes see of themselves and for their own sake; the special function of each part of the body can be attributed to the whole. And those functions which belong to a particular member by virtue of its nature can be said to be performed by the body which is the whole, so that the whole may properly be said to manifest the activity of its parts and the part that of the whole. That is why St. Paul's tongue could truthfully say: 'I suffer trouble in Christ's gospel even unto bonds,' (2 Tim. ii, 9) although his tongue was not itself in chains; and he goes on to say: 'The word of God is not bound.' Peter and John ran to Christ's sepulchre, although it was only their feet which performed the act of running; Stephen saw the heavens opened, although seeing is the special function of the eyes. Isaac touched and felt his son Jacob, yet the power of touching and feeling belongs particularly to the hands. And so it is clear that any action of an individual member is the work of the whole body; and conversely each of the parts participates in the action of the body as a whole.

For Reflection

1. Define *mystery* both in everyday terms and as Peter Damian understands it.

2. What does it mean that the Church is both one and many at the same time? What significance does this hold for you?

3. How do you participate in the whole Church? How is the entire Church shown in you?

5 Christ's Presence in the Church

Introduction

It has often been said that you can learn more about yourself from acquaintances than from immediate family members, who are either too close to you or too reluctant to tell the truth. Such may be the case with Simone Weil, a French Jew born to an agnostic family in 1909. Weil studied the classics of Greek and Roman literature and was reared in a liberal humanistic environment. Yet despite the influence of Marxism and Greek philosophers, she seems to have been graced with an innate love of God and a religious sensibility that drew her to Roman Catholicism. From this double perspective of secular, even atheistic, studies and her own religious intuition, she was able to appreciate the beauty and **sacramentality** of the Church, as reflected in many of her letters and essays. Her education and background also gave her the ability to offer constructive criticism of the Church when she found it too closed within itself or failing in its mission to preach the Good News.

There is an endearing but fundamental characteristic of Weil's personal spirituality—that of "waiting upon truth"—that may provide a partial answer to the question that many have asked since her death in 1943: Given her fervent love of Christ, the Sacraments, and the teachings of the Church, why was she never baptized a Christian? Undoubtedly, this characteristic of her spirituality was also part of her personality. For example, "waiting upon truth" can be explained by quoting from one of her essays on education: "In every school exercise there is a special way of waiting

sacramentality God's grace permeating the Church's life in all of its actions, not just the Seven Sacraments.

upon truth, setting our hearts upon it, yet not allowing ourselves to go out in search of it. There is a way of giving our attention to the data of a problem in geometry without trying to find the solution or to the words of a Latin or Greek text without trying to arrive at the meaning, a way of waiting, when we are writing, for the right word to come of itself. . . ." In fact, what Weil tried to do was to "wait upon truth" from God, discerning God's call so that she could be certain that accepting Baptism was the right thing for her to do. That she was never certain is a testament to the seriousness with which she took the Sacrament. She also thought that being on the outside allowed her to see what was most "catholic," or universal, about the Church and its practices. By not being too close, she believed she could see what others may have overlooked.

The selection in this chapter is from an essay entitled "Forms of the Implicit Love of God," in which Weil reflects on Christ's presence in the Church and in the Eucharist. It is remarkable for its theological insight and its view of Christ's presence from a wider, sociological perspective. Its core value lies in its expression of deep faith in the Church and in the Eucharist, which the writer fully affirms in the faith-offering of her writing.

Note: In this and other essays in this book, the words *man* and *men* are used in a universal sense, meaning both men and women.

Excerpt from *Waiting for God*
By Simone Weil

The virtue of religious practices is due to a contact with what is perfectly pure, resulting in the destruction of evil. Nothing here below is perfectly pure except the total beauty of the universe, and that we are unable to feel directly until we are very far advanced in the way of perfection. Moreover, this total beauty cannot be contained in anything tangible, though it is itself tangible in a certain sense.

Religious things are special tangible things, existing here below and yet perfectly pure. This is not on account of their own particular character.

> **Convention**
>
> A convention is an agreement about basic principles. For example, a literary convention is long-established technique, practice, or device upon which everyone agrees. (Beginning letters with *Dear* is a literary convention.) In Weil's description of the Eucharist as a "convention . . . ratified by God," she is stating that the Eucharist is truly the Body and Blood of Christ, not because bread is naturally associated with God but because of God's agreement with us to come to us in this mediated way, through sacramental symbols.

The church may be ugly, the singing out of tune, the priest corrupt, and the faithful inattentive. In a sense that is of no importance. It is as with a geometrician who draws a figure to illustrate a proof. If the lines are not straight and the circles are not round it is of no importance. Religious things are pure by right, theoretically, hypothetically, by convention. Therefore their purity is unconditioned. No stain can sully it. That is why it is perfect. It is not, however, perfect in the same way as **Roland's mare**, which, while it had all possible virtues, had also the drawback of not existing. Human conventions are useless if they are not connected with motives that impel people to observe them. In themselves they are simple abstractions; they are unreal and have no effect. But the convention by which religious things are pure is ratified by God himself. Thus it is an effective convention, a convention containing virtue and operating of itself. This purity is unconditioned and perfect, and at the same time real.

There we have a truth that is a fact and in consequence cannot be demonstrated by argument. It can only be verified experimentally.

It is a fact that the purity of religious things is almost everywhere to be seen in the form of beauty, when faith and love do not fail. Thus the words of the liturgy are marvelously beautiful; and the words of the prayer issued for us from the very lips of Christ is perfect above all. In the same way Romanesque architecture and Gregorian plain chant are marvelously beautiful.

At the very center, however, there is something utterly stripped of beauty, where there is no outward evidence of purity, something depending wholly on convention. It cannot be otherwise. Architecture, singing, language, even if the words are chosen by Christ himself, all those things are in a sense distinct from absolute purity. Absolute purity, present here below to our earthly senses, as a particular thing, such can only be a convention, which is a convention and nothing

> 66 *There is nothing in a morsel of bread that can be associated with our thought of God. Thus the conventional character of the divine presence is evident. Christ can be present in such an object only by convention. For this very reason he can be perfectly present in it.* 99

else. This convention, placed at the central point, is the Eucharist.

The virtue of the dogma of the **real presence** lies in its very absurdity. Except for the infinitely touching symbolism of food, there is nothing in a morsel of bread that can be associated with our thought of God. Thus the conventional character of the divine presence is evident. Christ can be present in such an object only by convention. For this very reason he can be perfectly present in it. God can only be present in secret here below. His presence in the Eucharist is truly secret since no part of our thought can reach the secret. Thus it is total.

No one dreams of being surprised that reasoning worked out from nonexistent perfect lines and perfect circles should be effectively applied to engineering. Yet that is incomprehensible. The reality of the divine presence in the Eucharist is more marvelous but not more incomprehensible.

One might in a sense say by analogy that Christ is present in the consecrated host by hypothesis, in the same way that a geometrician says by hypothesis that there are two equal angles in a certain triangle.

It is because it has to do with a convention that only the form of the consecration matters, not the spiritual state of him who consecrates.

Roland's mare A legendary horse that appears in the *Chanson de Roland*, a late eleventh- to early twelfth-century French epic poem about Roland, a military commander under Charlemagne (reigned AD 768–814).

Real Presence The true presence of Christ in the Eucharist under the species or appearances of bread and wine.

If it were something other than a convention, it would be at least partially human and not totally divine. A real convention is a supernatural harmony, taking the word harmony in the Pythagorean sense.

Only a convention can be the perfection of purity here below, for all nonconventional purity is more or less imperfect. That a convention should be real, that is a miracle of divine mercy.

For Reflection

1. Have you ever had a less than perfect experience of liturgy but encountered the Risen Christ anyway? Describe your experience.

2. In referring to Christ's presence in the Eucharist, Weil states, "That a convention should be real, that is a miracle of divine mercy." What does she mean by this?

3. Name one time when you "waited upon truth." What was it like?

6 "More Closely Bound"

Introduction

The Sacrament of Confirmation confers "special strength" from the Holy Spirit and makes a baptized Catholic "more closely bound to the Church."[1] This means that a confirmed Catholic becomes a full member of the Body of Christ and can enjoy the privileges of the Catholic faith: the opportunity to participate in various ministries and to exercise leadership in the parish community. Confirmation also carries responsibilities that last a lifetime. These, listed below, are extremely important for the Church as a whole and for each individual's walk with Christ. What are they? Those celebrating the Sacrament "are more strictly obliged to spread and defend the faith, both by word and by deed, as true witnesses of Christ."[2]

Spreading the faith is about evangelization. This means knowing the Catholic faith, knowing Christ, and sharing that knowledge with others. It's not proselytizing, because in evangelization we respect others' beliefs and opinions, but it is telling the faith story of the dying-death-Resurrection of Christ and what that means at school, at work, and among friends and family. Evangelization is the lived reality of having faith, including struggles, doubts, and unanswered questions. Defending the faith is the same thing. It's about explaining to others a way of life that makes the most sense, a way of life based on love, respect, and justice. This is often a countercultural message, so all Christians must be prepared for the disapproval that may come from others, even loved ones. Perhaps the most important point of the message of Confirmation is that evangelization is done by word and deed: not merely talking about faith but also living it. In *Evangelization in the Modern World* (*Evangelii Nuntiandi*, 1975), Pope Paul VI (1963–1978) said that people today are more willing to listen to the Word of God if it is lived rather than preached. Because this Pope shepherded the Church during years of the modern Church after Vatican Council II (1962–1965), he was responsible for implementing the decrees of that Council, many of which included the renewal of sacramental theology and of the rites of the Sacraments. In this introduction to the Rite of the Sacrament of Confirmation, Paul VI draws on the history of the celebration of this Sacrament, and describes the way in which it should be celebrated by the Church.

In his introduction, Paul VI outlines two theologies of Confirmation (initiation and maturation). He begins with a beautiful quote from Tertullian, a third-century theologian, recalls the scriptural roots of the Sacrament, outlines its history in the understanding and teaching of the Church, and then describes the actual rite in which the person is anointed with holy Chrism, or blessed oil. In the act of anointing with Chrism, the individual receives the Holy Spirit and is empowered to witness to Christ "by word and by deed." Anointing was used in the Old Testament to confer special status on kings and priests and to describe the deliverance of Israel from its oppressors in the person of a Messiah, or Anointed One, which is also the meaning of the Greek word *Christos,* or Christ. Throughout the Gospels Jesus is referred to as the Anointed One.

Note the special attention given to the words and actions of the Rite of Confirmation, printed in capital letters at the end of this excerpt. In every Sacrament both the words and the actions are essential to its celebration. Through the words and actions of the bishop (or a priest with special permission), Confirmation continues the saving work of God in the name of Christ through the power of the Holy Spirit begun at Pentecost.

Excerpt from "Apostolic Constitution on the Sacrament of Confirmation"

By Pope Paul VI

PAUL, BISHOP

Servant of the Servants of God For an Everlasting Memorial

The sharing in the divine nature received through the grace of Christ bears a certain likeness to the origin, development, and nourishing of natural life. The faithful are born anew by baptism, strengthened by the sacrament of confirmation, and finally are sustained by the food of eternal life in the eucharist. By means of these sacraments of Christian initiation, they thus receive in increasing measure the treasures of divine life and advance toward the perfection of charity. It has rightly been written: "The body is washed, that the soul may be cleansed; the body is anointed, that the soul may be consecrated; the body is signed, that the soul too may be fortified; the body is overshadowed by the laying on of hands, that the soul may be enlightened by the Spirit; the body is fed on the body and blood of Christ, that the soul may be richly nourished by God."[1] . . .

The New Testament shows how the Holy Spirit was with Christ to bring the Messiah's mission to fulfillment. On receiving the baptism of John, Jesus saw the Spirit descending on him (see Mk 1:10) and remaining with him (see Jn 1:32). He was led by the Spirit to undertake his public ministry as the Messiah, relying on the Spirit's presence and assistance. Teaching the people of Nazareth, he showed by what he said that the words of Isaiah, "The Spirit of the Lord is upon me," referred to himself (see Lk 4:17–21).

He later promised his disciples that the Holy Spirit would help them also to bear fearless witness to their faith even before persecutors (see Lk 12:12). The day before he suffered, he assured his apostles that he would send the Spirit of truth from his Father (see Jn 15:26) to stay with them "for ever" (Jn 14:16) and help them to be his witnesses (see Jn 15:26). Finally, after his resurrection, Christ promised the coming descent of the Holy Spirit: "You will receive power when the Holy Spirit comes upon you; then you are to be my witnesses" (Acts 1:8; see Lk 24:49).

On the feast of Pentecost, the Holy Spirit did indeed come down in an extraordinary way on the apostles as they were gathered together with Mary the mother of Jesus and the group of disciples. They were so "filled with" the Holy Spirit (Acts 2:4) that by divine inspiration they began to proclaim "the mighty works of God." Peter regarded the Spirit who had thus come down upon the apostles as the gift of the Messianic age (see Acts 2:17–18). Then those who believed the apostles' preaching were baptized and they too received "the gift of the Holy Spirit" (Acts 2:38). From that time on the apostles, in fulfillment of Christ's wish, imparted to the newly baptized by the laying on of hands the gift of the Spirit that completes the grace of baptism. This is why the Letter to the Hebrews listed among the first elements of Christian instruction the teaching about baptisms and the laying on of hands (Heb 6:2). This laying on of hands is rightly recognized by reason of Catholic tradition as the beginning of the sacrament of confirmation, which in a certain way perpetuates the grace of Pentecost in the Church.

> 66 *This laying on of hands is rightly recognized by reason of Catholic tradition as the beginning of the sacrament of confirmation, which in a certain way perpetuates the grace of Pentecost in the Church.* 99

This makes clear the specific importance of confirmation for sacramental initiation, by which the faithful "as members of the living Christ are incorporated into him and configured to him through baptism and through confirmation and the eucharist."[2] In baptism, the newly baptized receive forgiveness of sins, adoption as children of God, and the character of Christ by which they are made members of the Church and for the first time become sharers in the priesthood of their Savior (see 1 Pt 2:5, 9). Through the sacrament of confirmation those who have been born anew in baptism receive the inexpressible Gift, the Holy Spirit himself, by whom "they are endowed . . . with special strength."[3] Moreover, having been signed with the character of this sacrament, they are "more closely bound to the Church"[4] and "they are more strictly obliged to spread and defend the faith, both by word and by deed, as true witnesses of Christ."[5] Finally, confirmation is so closely linked with the holy eucharist[6] that the faithful, after being signed by baptism and confirmation, are incorporated fully into the Body of Christ by participation in the Eucharist.[7]

. . .

Our predecessor Innocent III wrote: "The anointing of the forehead with chrism signifies the laying on of the hand, the other name for which is confirmation, since through it the Holy Spirit is given for growth and strength."[8] Another of our predecessors, Innocent IV, mentions that the apostles conferred the Holy Spirit "through the laying on of the hand, which confirmation or the anointing of the forehead with chrism represents."[9] In the profession of faith of Emperor Michael Palaeologus read at the Council of Lyons II mention is made of

> ### The Celebration of Confirmation
>
> Two Ecumenical Councils noted by Pope Paul VI provide insight into the celebration of Confirmation. The Second Council of Lyons (1274) was the fourteenth Ecumenical Council. It was convened by Pope Gregory X and dealt with reunion of the Latin (Western) Church with the Greek (Eastern) Churches, achieved temporarily. The Council of Florence (1439–1445) was the seventeenth Ecumenical Council. This Council reaffirmed that the Holy Spirit proceeds from the Father and the Son and that there are seven Sacraments in the Church.

the sacrament of confirmation, which "bishops confer by the laying on of hands, anointing with chrism those who have been baptized."[10] The Decree for the Armenians, issued by the Council of Florence, declares that the "matter" of the sacrament of confirmation is "chrism made of olive oil . . . and balsam"[11] and, quoting the words of the Acts of the Apostles concerning Peter and John, who gave the Holy Spirit through the laying on of hands (see Acts 8:17), it adds: "in the Church in place of that laying on the hand, confirmation is given."[12] The Council of Trent, though it had no intention of defining the essential rite of confirmation, designated it simply by the term "the holy chrism of confirmation."[13] Benedict XIV made this declaration: "Therefore let this be said, which is beyond dispute: in the Latin Church the sacrament of confirmation is conferred by using the sacred chrism or olive oil mixed with balsam and blessed by the bishop, and by the sacramental minister's tracing the sign of the cross on the forehead of the recipient, while the same minister pronounces the words of the form."[14] . . .

THE SACRAMENT OF CONFIRMATION IS CONFERRED THROUGH THE ANOINTING WITH CHRISM ON THE FORE-HEAD, WHICH IS DONE BY THE LAYING ON OF THE HAND, AND THROUGH THE WORDS: BE SEALED WITH THE GIFT OF THE HOLY SPIRIT.[15]

Endnotes

1. Tertullian, De resurrection mortuorum 8, 3: CCL 2, 931.
2. Ad Gentes no. 36.
3. Lumen Gentium no. 11.
4. Ibid.
5. Ibid. See also Ad Gentes no. 11.
6. See Presbyterorum Ordinis no. 5.
7. See ibid.
8. Innocent III, Ep. "Cum venisset": PL 215, 285. The profession of faith that the same Pope imposed on the Waldenses has these words: "We regard confirmation by the bishop, that is, the laying on of hands, to be holy and to be received with reverence": PL 215, 1511.
9. Innocent IV, EP. "Sub Catholicae professione": Mansi 23, 579.
10. Council of Lyons II: Mansi 24, 71.
11. Epistolae Pontificiae ad I: Concilium Florentinum spectantes: C. Hofmann, ed., Concilium Florentinum v. 1, ser. A, part II (Rome, 1944) 128.
12. Ibid, 129.
13. Council of Trent 5, Act. II, 996.
14. Benedict XIV, Ep. "Ex quo primum tempore" 52: Benedicti XIV . . . Bullarium, v. 3 (Prati, 1847) 320.
15. Latin: ACCIPE SIGNACULUM DONI SPIRITUS SANCTI.

For Reflection

1. What New Testament references to the Holy Spirit does Pope Paul VI recall in this introduction to the Rite of Confirmation?

2. What historical evidence can be given for the presence of Confirmation as a Sacrament in the Church?

3. What does "special strength" mean to you, and how could it make a real difference in your life?

4. If you were asked to sponsor someone in Confirmation, what would you say and how would you prepare yourself and the person being confirmed for the Sacrament?

Part 2
Images of the Church

7 The Church as Mystery

Introduction

As discussed in chapter 4, "The Body of the Church," mystery is not an unsolved riddle or puzzle but the quality of our being, a quality that opens us to the presence and love of God in our lives. As we step back from the immediacy of daily living—classes, homework, deadlines—we become attentive to ourselves and other people. We begin to see life in a different way, not in a utilitarian or mechanistic sense (A causes B, which leads to C), but in a more integrated way from a higher perspective. From this higher perspective, we can see the beauty of existence and our role in it, which God has called us to and no other person can fulfill. By plumbing the depths of our own mystery and thereby losing ourselves in it, we find God, and by finding God, we find ourselves again: our true selves.

Matthias Joseph Scheeben (1835–1888), a German priest and author of *The Mysteries of Christianity* (1865), described mystery as a reaching down to the "innermost depths" of something to find its "ultimate essence." For him mystery was not about information but about being. All beings are mysterious, therefore, because no one can know their ultimate essence ex-

> **Predestination**
>
> As used by Scheeben, *predestination* is a theological concept taken from Romans 8:28–30, where Saint Paul recounts the process by which we are saved from sin and death: God *knows* us, *predestines* us from before our birth, *calls* us after our birth, *justifies* us as we live out our calling, and, finally, *glorifies* us with eternal life. Those who cooperate with God's grace, Saint Paul tells us, "are called according to his purpose" (v. 28). They are predestined.

cept God, their creator. Scheeben identified nine Christian
mysteries: Trinity, creation, sin,
Christ's Incarnation, the Eucharist, Church, glorification,
justification, and predestination.
He then described the work
of theology as the scientific
analysis and synthesis of these
mysteries, thus making them
understandable and accessible
to the wider Church.

In the selection that follows, Scheeben defines *mystery*
and then draws an important
theological distinction between

> **Revelation**
>
> *Revelation* refers to truth that is
> revealed by God and expressed
> through Scripture, liturgy,
> the teachings of the Church,
> and the witness of the saints.
> As Scheeben states, it cannot
> be attained through human
> reason. Contrast this with sci-
> entific truth, which is reached
> through trial and error and the
> systematic analysis of creation
> (i.e., the scientific method),
> and artistic truth, which is cre-
> ative insight and expression.

mystery in general and Christian mysteries in particular. The former
are mysteries that can be understood by human reason alone
without the need of religious faith. Examples of this abound in the
physical and natural sciences, as well as in philosophy. For Scheeben even the question of the existence of God is not a specifically
Christian mystery, because it can be grasped conceptually without
recourse to Divine Revelation. In other words, one doesn't have
to be a Christian to argue for or against the existence of a divine
being. However, Christian mysteries like the Eucharist cannot be
understood by human reason alone. Understanding depends on
God's grace through the gift of faith. This distinction was extremely
important to Scheeben because, as a theologian and professor, he
was involved in applying the science of theology to everyday faith.
It is important to us as
well, because as we real-
ize the limits of reason,
we have all the more in-
centive to open ourselves
to the mystery of faith.

justification God's action of bringing a
sinful human being into right relationship with him. It involves removal of sin
and the gift of God's sanctifying grace to
renew holiness.

Excerpt from *The Mysteries of Christianity*
By Matthias Joseph Scheeben

If by mystery we mean nothing more than an object which is not entirely conceivable and fathomable in its innermost essence, we need not seek very far to find mysteries. Such mysteries are found not only above us, but all around us, in us, under us. The real essence of all things is concealed from our eyes. The physicist will never fully plumb the laws of forces in the physico-chemical world and perfectly comprehend their effects; and the same is true of the physiologist with regard to the laws of organic nature, of the psychologist with regard to the soul, of the metaphysician with regard to the ultimate basis of all being.

Christianity is not alone in exhibiting mysteries in the above, mentioned sense. If its truths are inconceivable and unfathomable, so in greater part are the truths of reason. This by itself does not imply anything against Christianity, nor does it imply much in its favor. As will be shown, however, the truths that are specifically proper to Christianity are inconceivable and unfathomable in an exclusively special sense. To appreciate this fact, we must go on to consider another aspect of the notion of mystery.

When a person understands a truth, it is no longer a mystery for him but is clear to him, to the extent that he understands it. But do we not ordinarily say that he who understands a truth which he had not previously been aware of and did not suspect, or which others are not yet aware of, knows a secret or mystery? That is so; still, the truth is no longer a mystery for him. Well then, what if he were of himself utterly incapable of discovering the truth which he now knows, and which even now, after it has become manifest to him, is known only because another to whom he

> 66 *Mystery in its absolute form, as we have just described it, is Christian mystery, that is, mystery which divine revelation in the person of the incarnate Word proposes to the world for belief.* 99

lends credence has communicated it to him, and which, finally, even now he does not grasp by the light of his own intellect but only by faith? In this case the truth, in spite of such revelation, still remains hidden, because it does not lie open to our scrutiny and is not perceived in itself. If, in addition, the truth which has been revealed by another has absolutely no similarity, or but very slight similarity, with anything which we ourselves have ever seen or experienced, then naturally we are much less capable of forming a clear idea of it than we are of other things which do not extend beyond our experience. Thus in a double respect it will be obscure in its own way even after it has been revealed, and accordingly will be and will remain a mystery in a quite special sense.

Mysteries of this sort are, to some extent, found even in the natural order. Let us suppose, for instance, that a traveler from a foreign country, to which we cannot go, gives us an account of a plant whose color, blossom, and fragrance have practically no similarity with any we have seen; or that someone should discourse on light and its effects to a man born blind. In such cases, of course, the mystery is not absolute, and does not obtain for all men, since it is not at all obscure for some, or even for a large number. But let us take a truth to which no men, no creatures at all can attain by the natural means of cognition at their disposal, which they can perceive only by a supernatural illumination, which can be grasped only by belief in God's word, and which is remote from everything that the creature naturally knows, as remote as heaven is from earth. Then we have a mystery in its absolute form as a truth whose existence the creature cannot ascertain without belief in God's word, and whose subject matter he cannot represent and conceive directly, but only indirectly by comparison with dissimilar things.

Mystery in its absolute form, as we have just described it, is Christian mystery, that is, mystery which divine revelation in the person of the incarnate Word proposes to the world for belief.

In accordance with our description, two elements are essential to a mystery: first, that the existence of the proposed truth is attainable by no natural means of cognition, that it lies beyond the range of the created intellect; secondly, that its content is capable of apprehension only by

analogous concepts. If either one of these two elements is lacking, a truth cannot be called a mystery of Christianity in the strict sense, even if it has actually been proposed by Christian revelation. Owing to the absence of the first element, the doctrine of the existence of God and His essential attributes, for example, is not a mystery in this sense. For, although we apprehend all this only by analogous concepts, so that our notion must always remain obscure, reason can know that the objects apprehended really exist. Conversely, we are aware of many of God's works only through divine revelation (for example, the establishment of the Church as a juridical society pertaining to divine right, **prescinding** from its interior, supernatural character), the abstract notion of which, however, presents no special difficulty, because such things are similar to objects of our natural perception. Hence they are not mysteries in the narrower sense.

Mystery is generally defined as a truth concerning which we know that it is, but not how it is; that is, according to the usual explanation, we know that the subject and the predicate are really connected, but we are unable to determine and perceive the manner of the association.

This definition, if rightly explained, agrees in essentials with ours as given above. But it requires a detailed clarification, which is explicitly contained in our definition, and is not sufficiently expressed in the customary explanation.

Hence we shall do well to adhere to our definition, which is in no need of all these explanations and supplementary qualifications. In simpler form we can phrase it thus: Christian mystery is a truth communicated to us by Christian revelation, a truth to which we cannot attain by our unaided reason, and which, even after we have attained to it by faith, we cannot adequately represent with our rational concepts.

analogous From *analogy*; similar to or like something else.

prescinding Setting aside, leaving out of consideration.

For Reflection

1.   Scheeben states that ". . . the truths that are specifically proper to Christianity are inconceivable and unfathomable in an exclusively special sense." What does he mean by this?

2.   Scheeben claims that "two elements are essential to a mystery." What are they?

3.   Scheeben identifies the Church as a Christian mystery. Explain how the Church meets his "two elements" criterion for a Christian mystery.

8 The Church as Body

Introduction

The First Letter to the Corinthians may be the best-known of the Pauline Epistles of the New Testament. Its author, Saint Paul the Apostle, was a former Jewish religious leader who, in a unique encounter with the Risen Christ, became a Christian and then a leader and pillar of the Church. Paul's background and experience gave him a unique perspective on the Church's relationship to Christ. In the vision that resulted in his conversion, Paul heard Jesus, identifying himself with his followers, ask, "Why are you persecuting me?" (Acts of the Apostles 9:4).

In 1 Corinthians, from which you will read an excerpt in this chapter, Saint Paul uses imagery of the body to identify Jesus with his followers and to describe the Church as the Body of Christ. Like his other letters, 1 Corinthians begins by addressing practical problems. The church at Corinth, which was a thriving city on a trade route in Ancient Greece, had become splintered over issues concerning the Eucharist, marriage, sexual conduct, and Baptism. Paul admonished community members to follow "a still more excellent way" (12:31) by being faithful to Christ's message about the coming Reign of God and living in harmony with one another. This included properly understanding the Eucharist as the Body and Blood of Christ, not participating in activities that could cause scandal to those whose faith was weak, and developing what we would now call a spirituality or lifestyle

Gifts of the Holy Spirit These have been defined as seven: wisdom, understanding, knowledge, counsel, fortitude or courage, piety or reverence, and fear or awe of God. See Isaiah 11:2–3.

of love. Thus, for Paul, practical problems become springboards to comprehensive explanations of Christianity itself.

Another problem at Corinth involved members' quarreling over spiritual gifts. Paul responded by saying that there are many gifts, from wisdom and knowledge to healing, prophecy, and speaking in tongues (see 1 Corinthians 12:4–11). No gift is better than any other; they are merely different, and all help to build up the community. They have their source in the Holy Spirit, who infuses the community with love and unity (see 12:11). (Seven particular gifts have been traditionally grouped as the **Gifts of the Holy Spirit**.) In the same way, a body has different parts, but no part is greater than any other. All parts of the body need one another for the proper and complete functioning of the body. The Church, Paul says, is the Body of Christ. Through the Church, in the power of the Holy Spirit, Christ is present in the world. Just as the body needs all its parts, so the Body of Christ needs all its individual members to exercise their gifts together and thus give glory to God.

A final point, not in the reading but underscoring much of Pauline theology, is the importance of the Incarnation—God's being enfleshed in human form so that humanity might be saved from its sins and perfected in its holiness. This understanding of Incarnation is central to an understanding of life within the Church, the Body of Christ, and to approaching the Eucharist in what Paul would consider a "worthy" manner (see 11:27), recognizing the Body of Christ not only in the Eucharist but also in one another as members of Christ's Body, the Church.

Excerpt from the First Letter to the Corinthians

By Saint Paul the Apostle

From Chapter 11
Tradition of the Institution

For I received from the Lord what I also handed on to you, that the Lord Jesus, on the night he was handed over, took bread, and, after he had given thanks, broke it and said, "This is my body that is for you. Do this in remembrance of me." In the same way also the cup, after supper, saying, "This cup is the new covenant in my blood. Do this, as often as you drink it, in remembrance of me." For as often as you eat this bread and drink the cup, you proclaim the death of the Lord until he comes.

Therefore whoever eats the bread or drinks the cup of the Lord unworthily will have to answer for the body and blood of the Lord. A person should examine himself, and so eat the bread and drink the cup. For anyone who eats and drinks without discerning the body, eats and drinks judgment on himself. That is why many among you are ill and infirm, and a considerable number are dying. If we discerned ourselves, we would not be under judgment; but since we are judged by [the] Lord, we are being disciplined so that we may not be condemned along with the world.

Therefore, my brothers, when you come together to eat, wait for one another. If anyone is hungry, he should eat at home, so that your meetings may not result in judgment. The other matters I shall set in order when I come.

Chapter 12
Unity and Variety

Now in regard to spiritual gifts, brothers, I do not want you to be unaware. You know how, when you were pagans, you were constantly attracted and led away to mute idols. Therefore, I tell you that nobody speaking by the spirit of God says, "Jesus be accursed." And no one can say, "Jesus is Lord," except by the holy Spirit.

There are different kinds of spiritual gifts but the same Spirit; there are different forms of service but the same Lord; there are different workings but the same God who produces all of them in everyone. To each individual the manifestation of the Spirit is given for some benefit. To one is given through the Spirit the expression of wisdom; to another the expression of knowledge according to the same Spirit; to another faith by the same Spirit; to another gifts of healing by the one Spirit; to another mighty deeds; to another prophecy; to another discernment of spirits; to another varieties of tongues; to another interpretation of tongues. But one and the same Spirit produces all of these, distributing them individually to each person as he wishes.

One Body, Many Parts

As a body is one though it has many parts, and all the parts of the body, though many, are one body, so also Christ. For in one Spirit we were all baptized into one body, whether Jews or Greeks, slaves or free persons, and we were all given to drink of one Spirit.

Now the body is not a single part, but many. If a foot should say, "Because I am not a hand I do not belong to the body," it does not for this reason belong any less to the body. Or if an ear should say, "Because I am not an eye I do not belong to the body," it does not for this reason belong any less to the body. If the whole body were an eye, where would the hearing be? If the whole body were hearing, where would the sense of smell be? But as it is, God placed the parts, each one of them, in

> " *To each individual the manifestation of the Spirit is given for some benefit.* "

the body as he intended. If they were all one part, where would the body be? But as it is, there are many parts, yet one body. The eye cannot say to the hand, "I do not need you," nor again the head to the feet, "I do not need you."

Indeed, the parts of the body that seem to be weaker are all the more necessary, and those parts of the body that we consider less honorable we surround with greater honor, and our less presentable parts are treated

> **Speaking in Tongues**
>
> This spiritual gift is some-times called *glossolalia*, a Greek compound of *glossa* (tongue or language) and *laleo* (first person indicative of "to speak" or "ramble"). This gift of offering praise in an unintelligible language is still active in charismatic groups. Saint Paul mentions that this is a valuable gift if it is accompanied by interpretation—that is, the gift of interpreting the speaker's words by community members (see 1 Corinthians 14:4–5).

with greater propriety, whereas our more presentable parts do not need this. But God has so constructed the body as to give greater honor to a part that is without it, so that there may be no division in the body, but that the parts may have the same concern for one another. If [one] part suffers, all the parts suffer with it; if one part is honored, all the parts share its joy.

Application to Christ

Now you are Christ's body, and individually parts of it. Some people God has designated in the church to be, first, apostles; second, prophets; third, teachers; then, mighty deeds; then, gifts of healing, assistance, administration, and varieties of tongues. Are all apostles? Are all prophets? Are all teachers? Do all work mighty deeds? Do all have gifts of healing? Do all speak in tongues? Do all interpret? Strive eagerly for the greatest spiritual gifts.

The Way of Love

But I shall show you a still more excellent way.

For Reflection

1. In 1 Corinthians, chapter 11, Paul describes the relationship between the Eucharist and the Body of Christ, the members of the Church. In your own words, describe this relationship.

2. What gifts have you been given as a member of the Body of Christ? How are you using these gifts? How do you foresee using them in the future?

3. How might you help others discern their gifts? How would doing so help not only them but also you?

4. Paul writes, "For in one Spirit we were all baptized into one body, whether Jews or Greeks, slaves or free persons, and we were all given to drink of one Spirit" (1 Corinthians 12:13). What does this mean for your parish or school community? What does it mean for you?

9 A Church in Exile

Introduction

We are not accustomed to think of the Church as being in exile. The Church was a global institution long before the word *globalization* ever became popular. It has a highly developed infrastructure and a history of direct involvement in public discourse. Its home is in society and the world, not apart from it. Yet the word *exile* conjures up images of being away from home, banished from everything familiar. Exile is a terrible hardship for anyone, especially a people, because exile is often a permanent condition with little hope of returning home to what once was, to the familiar places and events of the past. It may involve wandering aimlessly without a map or plan or fixed goal. If you examine the history of the Jews, including their enslavement in Egypt and exile in both Assyria and Babylonia, it becomes clear that exile has been an integral part of their identity as a people and their relationship with God. This is also true of the Church, the New People of God, which has suffered persecution and martyrdom throughout history. Is

> ### Assyrian and Babylonian Exiles
>
> The Assyrian and Babylonian Exiles were two separate conquests and forced exiles of the Jews, the first by the Assyrians (721 BC), which ended the Northern Kingdom of Israel, and the second by the Babylonians (605, 597, 587 BC). See 1 and 2 Kings and Ezra and Nehemiah for a historical account of the Exiles; Lamentations for poetry of grief and lament over exile; and the major prophetic books (Isaiah, Jeremiah, Ezekiel) for theological interpretations of the meaning of these events. The Babylonian Exile ended when King Cyrus of Babylon allowed the Jews to return home in 538 BC.

it possible that the Church was not meant to be a stable fixture in the world after all? Is exile a credible or accurate way of describing the Church today?

The bishops and other leaders gathered at the Second Vatican Council in Rome certainly thought so. In *Dogmatic Constitution on the Church,* titled *Lumen Gentium* ("the Light of Nations"), one of the images used for the Church is that of exile. *Lumen Gentium* draws a connection with the Old Testament by noting that "Israel according to the flesh, which wandered as an exile in the desert, was already called the Church of God. So likewise the new Israel which while living in this present age goes in search of a future and abiding city is called the Church of Christ" (9). Both Churches wander in exile while waiting with "groan and travail" to be called home to God the Father (48). Further, the bishops distinguished the things of this world from those of the next, exhorting the faithful not to become attached to riches but to rise above the distractions of the world and discover what truly satisfies the human heart.

The reading in this chapter is taken from several sections of *Lumen Gentium* but contains the same theme: the Church in this world is in exile. As members of the Church, we should not seek or depend on the comforts of this world nor be seduced by passing fads. Rather, we should strive to attain "perfect love" (42) by acting justly with others, picking up our crosses, and following Christ, who is our true home.

Second Vatican Council

Pope Saint John XXIII convened this twenty-first Ecumenical Council to bring the Church up to date with the modern world (*aggiornamento*). *Lumen Gentium* is one of only two dogmatic constitutions issued by the council (the other being *Dei Verbum*, "On Divine Revelation"). *Lumen Gentium* offered a distinctly new understanding of the Church not as a society or institution but as a "People of God . . . reborn not from a perishable but from an imperishable seed through the word of the living God, not from flesh but from water and the Holy Spirit" (9).

Excerpt from *Dogmatic Constitution on the Church (Lumen Gentium)*

By the Second Vatican Council

Chapter I: The Mystery of the Church

6. . . . The Church, further, "that Jerusalem which is above" is also called "our mother." (Gal. 4:26, cf. Rev. 12:17.) It is described as the spotless spouse of the spotless Lamb, (Rev.19:7; 21:2 and 9; 22:17) whom Christ "loved and for whom He delivered Himself up that He might sanctify her," (Eph. 5:26) whom He unites to Himself by an unbreakable covenant, and whom He unceasingly "nourishes and cherishes," (Eph. 5:29) and whom, once purified, He willed to be cleansed and joined to Himself, subject to Him in love and fidelity, (cf. Eph. 5:24) and whom, finally, He filled with heavenly gifts for all eternity, in order that we may know the love of God and of Christ for us, a love which surpasses all knowledge. (Cf. Eph. 3:19) The Church, while on earth it journeys in a foreign land away from the Lord, (Cf. 2 Cor. 5:6) is like in exile. It seeks and experiences those things which are above, where Christ is seated at the right-hand of God, where the life of the Church is hidden with Christ in God until it appears in glory with its Spouse. (Cf. Col. 3:1–4.) . . .

8. . . . Just as Christ carried out the work of redemption in poverty and persecution, so the Church is called to follow the same route that it might communicate the fruits of salvation to men. Christ Jesus, "though He was by nature God . . . emptied Himself, taking the nature of a slave," (Phil. 2:6) and "being rich, became poor" (2 Cor. 8:9) for our sakes. Thus, the Church, although it needs human resources to carry out its mission, is not set up to seek earthly glory, but to proclaim, even by its own example, humility and self-sacrifice. Christ was sent by the Father "to bring good news to the poor, to heal the contrite of heart," (Lk.4:18) "to seek and to save what was lost." (Lk.19:10) Similarly, the Church encompasses with love all who are afflicted with human suffering and in the poor and afflicted sees the image of its poor and suffering Founder. It does all it can to relieve their need and in them it strives to serve Christ. While Christ, holy, innocent and undefiled (Heb.7:26) knew nothing of

sin, (2 Cor. 5:21) but came to expiate only the sins of the people, (cf. Heb.2:17) the Church, embracing in its bosom sinners, at the same time holy and always in need of being purified, always follows the way of penance and renewal. The Church, "like a stranger

> *By the power of the risen Lord it [the Church] is given strength that it might, in patience and in love, overcome its sorrows and its challenges, both within itself and from without, and that it might reveal to the world, faithfully though darkly, the mystery of its Lord until, in the end, it will be manifested in full light.*

in a foreign land, presses forward amid the persecutions of the world and the consolations of God"[1] announcing the cross and "death of the Lord until He comes."(Cf. 1 Cor. 11:26.) By the power of the risen Lord it is given strength that it might, in patience and in love, overcome its sorrows and its challenges, both within itself and from without, and that it might reveal to the world, faithfully though darkly, the mystery of its Lord until, in the end, it will be manifested in full light. . . .

Chapter V: The Universal Call to Holiness

42. Therefore, all the faithful of Christ are invited to strive for the holiness and perfection of their own proper state. Indeed they have an obligation to so strive. Let all then have care that they guide aright their own deepest sentiments of soul. Let neither the use of the things of this world nor attachment to riches, which is against the spirit of **evangelical poverty**, hinder them in their quest for perfect love. Let them heed the admonition of the Apostle to those who use this world; let them not come to terms with this world; for this world, as we see it, is passing away. (Cf. 1 Cor. 7:31 ff.) . . .

Chapter VII: The Eschatological Nature of the Pilgrim Church and Its Union with the Church in Heaven

48. The Church, to which we are all called in Christ Jesus, and in which

evangelical poverty Literally meaning "Gospel poverty," a recognition of our deep need for God and the commitment to put God above everything else in life, particularly above the accumulation of material wealth.

we acquire sanctity through the grace of God, will attain its full perfection only in the glory of heaven, when there will come the time of the restoration of all things. (Acts 3:21) At that time the human race as well as the entire world, which is intimately related to man and attains to its end through him, will be perfectly reestablished in Christ. (Cf Eph. 1:10; Col. 1:20; 2 Pt. 3:10–13.)

Christ, having been lifted up from the earth has drawn all to Himself. (Cf. Jn. 12:32.) Rising from the dead (cf. Rom. 6:9) He sent His life-giving Spirit upon His disciples and through Him has established His Body which is the Church as the universal sacrament of salvation. Sitting at the right hand of the Father, He is continually active in the world that He might lead men to the Church and through it join them to Himself and that He might make them partakers of His glorious life by nourishing them with His own Body and Blood. Therefore the promised restoration which we are awaiting has already begun in Christ, is carried forward in the mission of the Holy Spirit and through Him continues in the Church in which we learn the meaning of our terrestrial life through our faith, while we perform with hope in the future the work committed to us in this world by the Father, and thus work out our salvation. (Cf. Phil. 2:12.)

Already the final age of the world has come upon us (cf. 1 Cor. 10:11) and the renovation of the world is irrevocably decreed and is already anticipated in some kind of a real way; for the Church already on this earth is signed with a sanctity which is real although imperfect. However, until there shall be new heavens and a new earth in which justice dwells, (cf. 2 Pt. 3:13) the pilgrim Church in her sacraments and institutions, which pertain to this present time, has the appearance of this world which is passing and she herself dwells among creatures who groan and travail in pain until now and await the revelation of the sons of God. (Cf. Rom. 8:19–22.)

Joined with Christ in the Church and signed with the Holy Spirit "who is the pledge of our inheritance," (Eph. 1:14) truly we are called and we are sons of God (cf. 1 Jn. 3:1) but we have not yet appeared with Christ in glory, (cf. Col. 3:4) in which we shall be like to God, since we shall see Him as He is. (Cf. 1 Jn. 3:2) And therefore "while we are in the body, we are exiled from the Lord (2 Cor. 5:6) and having the first-fruits of the Spirit we groan within ourselves (cf. Rom. 8:23) and we desire to be with Christ.'" (Cf. Phil. 1:23) By that same charity however, we are urged to live more for Him, who died for us and rose again. (Cf. 2 Cor. 5:15.) We strive therefore to please God in all things (cf. 2 Cor. 5:9) and we put on the armor of God, that we may be able to stand against the wiles of the devil and resist in the evil day. (Cf. Eph. 6:11–13.) Since however we know not the day nor the hour, on Our Lord's advice we must be constantly vigilant so that, having finished the course of our earthly life, (cf. Heb. 9:27) we may merit to enter into the marriage feast with Him and to be numbered among the blessed (cf. Mt. 25:31–46) and that we may not be ordered to go into eternal fire (cf. Mt. 25:41) like the wicked and slothful servant, (cf. Mt. 25:26) into the exterior darkness where "there will be the weeping and the gnashing of teeth." (Mt. 22:13 and 25:30) For before we reign with Christ in glory, all of us will be made manifest "before the tribunal of Christ, so that each one may receive what he has won through the body, according to his works, whether good or evil" (2 Cor. 5:10) and at the end of the world "they who have done good shall come forth unto resurrection of life; but those who have done evil unto resurrection of judgment." (Jn. 5:29; Cf. Mt. 25:46.) Reckoning therefore that "the sufferings of the present time are not worthy to be compared with the glory to come that will be revealed in us," (Rom. 8:18; cf. 2 Tim. 2:11–12) strong in faith we look for the "blessed hope and the glorious coming of our great God and Saviour, Jesus Christ" (Tit. 2:13) "who will refashion the body of our lowliness, conforming it to the body of His glory["] (Phil. 3:21), and who will come "to be glorified in His saints and to be marveled at in all those who have believed" (2 Thess. 1:10).

49. Until the Lord shall come in His majesty, and all the angels with Him (cf. Mt. 25:31) and death being destroyed, all things are subject to Him, (cf. Eph. 4:1–6) some of His disciples are exiles on earth, some having died are purified, and others are in glory beholding "clearly God Himself triune and one, as He is";[2] but all in various ways and degrees are in communion in the same charity of God and neighbor and all sing the same hymn of glory to our God. For all who are in Christ, having His Spirit, form one Church and cleave together in Him. (Cf. Eph. 4:16.) Therefore the union of the wayfarers with the brethren who have gone to

sleep in the peace of Christ is not in the least weakened or interrupted, but on the contrary, according to the perpetual faith of the Church, is strengthened by communication of spiritual goods. For by reason of the fact that those in heaven are more closely united with Christ, they establish the whole Church more firmly in holiness, lend nobility to the worship which the Church offers to God here on earth and in many ways contribute to its greater edification. (Cf. 1 Cor. 12:12–27.) For after they have been received into their heavenly home and are present to the Lord, (cf. 2 Cor. 5:8) through Him and with Him and in Him they do not cease to intercede with the Father for us, showing forth the merits which they won on earth through the one Mediator between God and man, (cf. 1 Tim. 2:5) serving God in all things and filling up in their flesh those things which are lacking of the sufferings of Christ for His Body which is the Church. (Cf. Col. 1:24.) Thus by their brotherly interest our weakness is greatly strengthened.

Endnotes

1. S. Augustinus, Civ. Dei, XVIII, 51, 2: PL 41, 614.
2. Conc. Florentinum, Decretum pro Graecis: Denz. 693 (1305).

For Reflection

1. If the Church exists in exile, what does that mean for its relationship with other societal institutions like government and business?

2. As a member of the Church, how might you live "in exile" while still engaging in relationships, social activities, and work?

3. *Lumen Gentium* describes holiness as being in touch with your "deepest sentiments" and guiding them "aright" (42). Given that description, how might you become more holy?

4. Do you think the Church places too much emphasis on "the glory to come" rather than "the sufferings of the present"? Why or why not?

10 A Community of Sinners

Introduction

Community is one of those things that sounds good in theory and looks good on paper, but actually living it can be a messy affair. Sharing space with other people may be the hardest thing for independent individuals to ever do and can be a source of great anguish but also of immeasurable blessing. Having roommates, going to summer camp, or otherwise sharing room and board with others highlights how challenging people can be, even friends and relatives. And even though, as noted in *Lumen Gentium* in the previous chapter, the Church is made up of the People of God, a chosen race, a royal priesthood, its members are still human beings with all of the foibles and imperfections that are attendant upon our race. Dorothy Day, a Roman Catholic activist and cofounder of the Catholic Worker movement, observed that the only thing that can get one through a day in community is "love and ever more love."

What did she mean by that? Simply, that our declarations of faith in Christ and commitment to others, particularly the poor and outcast (the exiled), are of little value if they remain purely conceptual; that is, if they are untested by life. John Milton (1608–1674), the British

> **Catholic Worker Movement**
>
> The Catholic Worker movement was cofounded by Dorothy Day and Peter Maurin in 1933 and is based on the corporal works of mercy and Catholic social justice teaching. The new social order espoused by both founders is centered on cooperating with God's grace in helping to make the Kingdom of God a lived reality here on Earth. More information can be found by searching "Catholic Worker" on the Internet.

romantic poet of the seventeenth century, considered "untried virtue" no virtue at all. It is easy to say, as did Peter, "Lord, I will never leave you" (see John 6:67–69), but it is only when challenged or threatened that we truly declare who and what we are. So it is with religious sentiment and beliefs. If they remain academic or intellectual endeavors, they are not real virtues. The theological virtues of faith, hope, and love are not theoretical niceties but the true test of individual character. As Saint Paul wrote in the First Letter to the Corinthians (see chapter 8), "If I speak in human and angelic tongues but do not have love, I am a resounding gong or a clashing cymbal" (13:1).

In the following piece, Dorothy Day writes about living with others and trying to guide them toward greater service to one another and toward love of Christ. It wasn't easy. She lived in a community of laypeople who were jobless and homeless. People were often on edge. Differing expectations regarding her role as leader also complicated the picture. The "new social order" she speaks of was the goal of the Catholic Worker movement, which she cofounded with Peter Maurin in 1933, during the Great Depression. Its goal was to effect change in the existing social structure through works of mercy. Since the time the first Catholic Worker house was founded in New York City, Catholic Worker houses have been established all over the world. They continue to provide shelter, clothing, and food to people in need.

As you read this selection, keep in mind the image of the Church as the Body of Christ. How does the lifestyle described here reflect that image, even incompletely?

Works of Mercy

Traditionally, these have been divided into spiritual and corporal works, seven of each. The spiritual works of mercy are admonishing the sinner, instructing the ignorant, counseling the doubtful, comforting the sorrowful, bearing injustice, forgiving injuries, and praying for the living and dead. The corporal works of mercy are feeding the hungry, giving drink to the thirsty, clothing the naked, sheltering the homeless, attending to the sick, visiting those in prison, and burying the dead (see *CCC*, 2447).

"Love and Ever More Love"

By Dorothy Day

Bernanos in his *Diary of a Country Priest* writes, "Hell is not to love any more."

I felt when I read this that the blackness of hell must indeed have descended on our Lord in His agony.

The one thing that makes our work easier most certainly is the love we bear for each other and for the people for whom we work. The work becomes difficult only when there is quarreling and dissension and when one's own heart is filled with a spirit of criticism.

In the past, when I have spoken on the necessity of mutual charity, of self-criticism rather than criticism of others, the accusation has been made that I talk to the men as though they were angels, that I do not see their faults. Which is certainly not true.

The difficulty for me is not in not seeing the other person's faults, but in seeing and developing his virtues. A community of lay people is entirely different from a religious community like the Benedictines. We must imitate them by thinking in terms of work and prayer. But we must always remember that those who come to us are not there voluntarily, many of them, but because of economic circumstances. They have taken refuge with us. There is the choice of being on the streets, taking city care such as it is, or staying with us. Even many of the young "leaders" who give up home and position to come to help in the work are the rebel type and often undisciplined. Their great virtues often mean correspondingly great faults.

Yet those who are interested in the movement fail to see why it does not run as smoothly as a religious movement. They expect our houses and farms to be governed as a religious community is ruled, and in general they take the attitude that I am the one in authority who should rule with an iron hand, the others accepting this willingly. Truly the position of authority is the difficult one.

One of the difficulties of the work is to find those who are willing to assume authority. Leaders are hard to find. The very best in our groups who are members of unions for instance, are steadfast, humble, filled with the love of God and their fellows, and their very virtues make it hard for them to assume leadership. Often, then, they leave it to the articulate ones who are often most articulate about the wrong doings. They leave the foremost positions to those who like to talk rather than to do, to those who are aggressive and pugnacious and who do the movement harm rather than good. If they are not saying the wrong thing, enunciating the wrong ideas—being politicians, in other words—then they are *saying* but not *doing,* and even doing contrary to what they are saying. . . .

It is human to dislike being found fault with. If you point out faults, rather than point out the better way of doing things, then the sting is there, and resentments and inactivity are the results. "What's the use of doing anything, it's all wrong!" Such childishness! But human beings are like that, and we must recognize their faults and try in every possible way to bring out their virtues.

On a visit to a group, there are always a halfdozen who are filled with complaints. . . . If you try to turn their criticisms so as to change their attitude of mind, you are refusing to listen to them. You don't give them a chance to show you how wrong everything is. You don't know what is going on. It is in vain that you assure them you do know what is going on, just how faulty different ones have been. No, that is not enough, if you treat all with equal patience, then you are not paying any attention to the complaints. Positive work to overcome obstacles such as people's temperaments is not enough for the fault-finders. They want recriminations and reprimands. "You are going to let him get away with that?" is the cry, when you try with courtesy and sympathy and respect to draw people together and induce cooperation.

It is very trying to receive so many complaints and not to be able to do anything about them. Those who do not complain and who try to work along the positive method are accused of being yes-men, and those who tell on each other and who always have some tale of woe, are informers. So in either case there is trouble. . . .

Oh yes, my dear comrades and fellow workers, I see only too clearly how bad things are with us all, how bad you all are, and how bad a leader I am. I see it only too often and only too clearly. It is because I see it so clearly that I must lift up my head and keep in sight the aims we must always hold before us. I must see the large and generous picture of the new social order wherein justice dwelleth. I must hold always in mind the new earth where God's Will will be done as it is in Heaven. I must hold it in mind for my own courage and for yours.

The new social order as it could be and would be if all men loved God and loved their brothers because they are all sons of God! A land of peace and tranquillity and joy in work and activity. It is Heaven indeed that we are contemplating. Do you expect that we are going to be able to accomplish it here? We can accomplish much, of that I am certain. We can do much to change the face of the earth, in that I have hope and faith. But these pains and sufferings are the price we have to pay. Can we change men in a night or a day? Can we give them as much as three months or even a year? A child is forming in the mother's womb for nine long months, and it seems so long. But to make a man in the time of our present disorder with all the world convulsed with hatred and strife and selfishness, that is a lifetime's work and then too often it is not accomplished.

Even the best of human love is filled with self-seeking. To work to increase our love for God and for our fellow man (and the two must go hand in hand), this is a life-time job. We are never going to be finished.

Love and ever more love is the only solution to every problem that comes up. If we love each other enough, we will bear with each other's faults and burdens. If we love enough, we are going to light that fire in the hearts of others. And it is love that will burn out the sins and hatreds that sadden us. It is love that will make us want to do great things for each other. No sacrifice and no suffering will then seem too much.

Yes, I see only too clearly how bad people are. I wish I did not see it so. It is my own sins that give me such clarity. If I

> 66 *Love and ever more love is the only solution to every problem that comes up. If we love each other enough, we will bear with each other's faults and burdens. If we love enough, we are going to light that fire in the hearts of others.* 99

did not bear the scars of so many sins to dim my sight and dull my capacity for love and joy, then I would see Christ more clearly in you all.

I cannot worry much about your sins and miseries when I have so many of my own. I can only love you all, poor fellow travelers, fellow sufferers. I do not want to add one least straw to the burden you already carry. My prayer from day to day is that God will so enlarge my heart that I will see you all, and live with you all, in His love.

For Reflection

1. How would you summarize the goals of the Catholic Worker movement as outlined by Dorothy Day? How does this and similar Catholic movements contribute to the life of the Church?

2. One of the themes in the text is leadership. How does Day describe her goals and methods of leadership? What is a leader and why do people follow him or her?

3. Do you agree that "if we love each other enough, we will bear with each other's faults and burdens"? Explain your answer.

4. Is this reading more about the community or Day herself? Explain your answer.

11 Mother Church and Mother Jesus

Introduction

In the early morning of May 13, 1373, a young woman lay feverish and dying in Norwich, England. The parish priest was sent for and last rites given. As she fixed her gaze upon the crucifix that the priest held before her, she prayed to God not to spare her life but to purify her faith and to bring her closer to God through her pain. God responded by giving this "simple creature unlettered," as she referred to herself, sixteen "Shewings" (visions or revelations) that she recorded and edited upon her recovery, which began immediately. These "Shewings" of Julian of Norwich have become famous in Christian spirituality for their appeal not only to religious and clergy but also to all Christians ("even-Christians"). They provide a vivid interpretation of Christ's Passion, as well as simple but wise advice about love: "Because of the Shewing I am not good but if I love God the better: and in as much as ye love God the better, it is more to you than me. I say not this

> **Contemplative Prayer**
>
> As distinguished from discursive and meditative prayer, both of which search for God through active means (speech or supplication in discursive prayer; meditation or reflection in meditative prayer), contemplative prayer is a form of mental prayer in which all active means cease. One does not search for God as much as empty oneself in order to be found by God. Famous contemplatives in the Catholic Christian tradition are Saint Teresa of Ávila (1515–1582) and Saint John of the Cross (1542–1591).

to them that be wise for they **wot** [know] it well; but I say it to you that be simple, for ease and comfort: for we are all one in comfort [love]."

Julian's visions are a form of contemplative prayer that brought her closer to God through the intensity of the images (she refers to Christ's blood, face, and wounds in detail) and her subsequent reflection on these images. She says she understood "six things" from her experience: the precious blood of Christ that was shed for humanity; the "Maiden" Mary; the Trinity as "Almighty, All-Wisdom, All-Love"; God as the "Maker of all things"; that God made all things for love and sustains them by love; and, finally, that God is goodness and that whatever good a creature has comes from God. She was also "stirred in charity to mine even-Christians, that they might see and know the same that I saw: for I would it were a comfort to them." In this way, Julian attempted to move the focus away from her visions as a personal experience of revelation so that others might benefit from them as if they were their own. From this we can see that Julian saw her gifts as benefitting the whole Body of Christ. Her message of God's love and care has been treasured by the Church in the ensuing centuries.

In the two excerpts that follow, Julian speaks of mother Jesus and mother Church, emphasizing the loving nature of both and emphasizing that humanity's true nature ("kynde") is not sinful. Sin, she believed, was due to a lack of wisdom rather than inner depravity. Not knowing who we are can lead to wrong decisions, which separate us from God, but in the pain resulting from sin we experience Christ's Passion and become one with him, which is the goal of contemplation. Finally, regarding the text, be aware that Julian writes in the Middle English of the fourteenth century, a time when English was heavily influenced

wit, wot, wist, witteth Variants meaning think, understand, know.

by French and Latin. You may be unfamiliar with certain spellings and syntax, but reading the original will give you a much better feel for both the woman and the "Shewings" from God.

Excerpts from *Revelations of Divine Love*
By Julian of Norwich

Chapter LX

. . . He might no more die, but He would not stint of working: wherefore then it behoveth Him to feed us; for the dearworthy love of Motherhood hath made Him debtor to us. The mother may give her child suck of her milk, but our precious Mother, Jesus, He may feed us with Himself, and doeth it, full courteously and full tenderly, with the Blessed Sacrament that is precious food of my life; and with all the sweet Sacraments He sustaineth us full mercifully and graciously. And so meant He in this blessed word where that He said: *It is I*[1] *that Holy Church preacheth thee and teacheth thee.* That is to say: *All the health and life of Sacraments, all the virtue and grace of my Word, all the Goodness that if ordained in Holy Church for thee, it is I.* The Mother may lay the child tenderly to her breast, but our tender Mother, Jesus, He may homely lead us into His blessed breast, by His sweet open side, and shew therein part of the Godhead and the joys of Heaven, with spiritual sureness of endless bliss. And that shewed He in the Tenth [Shewing], giving the same understanding in this sweet word

> **Nature**
>
> Julian uses the word *nature* in a beautifully harmonious way, relating it to goodness and describing it as both a state of being and an action. When we strive through the grace of God to do the morally right thing, to be disciples of Christ, we become more like God in our nature and are restored to righteousness in our being. God is the source for all that is good and holy in us. The image Julian uses is of flowing out of God, who is pure goodness, and then being poured back into God by grace and love.

where He saith: *Lo! how I loved thee;* looking unto [the Wound in] His side, rejoicing.

This fair lovely word *Mother,* it is so Sweet and so close in Nature of itself[2] that it may not verily be said of none but of *Him;* and to her that is very Mother of Him and of all. To the property of Motherhood belongeth natural love, wisdom, and knowing; and it is good: for though it be so that our bodily forthbringing be but little, low, and simple in regard of our spiritual forthbringing, yet it is He that doeth it in the creatures by whom that it is done. The Kindly,[3] loving Mother that witteth and knoweth the need of her child, she keepeth it full tenderly, as the nature and condition of Motherhood will. And as it **waxeth** in age, she changeth her working, but not her love. And when it is waxen of more age, she suffereth that it be beaten[4] in breaking down of vices, to make the child receive virtues and graces. This working, with all that be fair and good, our Lord doeth it in them by whom it is done: thus He is our Mother in Nature by the working of Grace in the lower part for love of the higher part. And He willeth that we know this: for He will have all our love fastened to Him. And in this I saw that all our duty that we owe, by God's bidding, to Fatherhood and Motherhood, for [reason of] God's Fatherhood and Motherhood is fulfilled in true loving of God; which blessed love Christ worketh in us. And this was shewed in all [the Revelations] and especially in the high plenteous words where He saith: *It is I that thou lovest.*

Chapter LXI

. . . The mother may suffer the child to fall sometimes, and to be hurt in diverse manners for its own profit, but she may never suffer that any manner of peril come to the child, for love. And though our earthly mother may suffer her child to perish, our heavenly Mother, Jesus, may not suffer us that are His children to perish: for He is All-mighty, All-wisdom, and All-love; and so is none but He,—blessed may He be!

But oftentimes when our falling and our wretchedness is shewed us, we are so sore **adread**, and so greatly ashamed of our self, that scarcely we find where we may hold us. But then willeth not our courteous Mother that we flee away, for Him were nothing **lother**. But He willeth then that we use the condition of a child: for when it is hurt, or adread, it runneth hastily to the mother for help, with all its might. So willeth He that we do, as a meek child saying thus: *My kind Mother, my Gracious Mother, my dearworthy Mother, have mercy on me: I have made myself foul and unlike to Thee, and I nor may nor can amend it but with thine help and grace.* And if we feel us not then eased forthwith, be we sure that He useth the condition of a wise mother. For if He see that it be more profit to us to mourn and to weep, He suffereth it, with **ruth** and pity, unto the best time, for love. And He willeth then that we use the property of a child, that evermore of nature trusteth to the love of the mother in weal and in woe.

And He willeth that we take us mightily to the Faith of Holy Church and find there our dearworthy Mother, in solace of true Understanding, with all the blessed Common. For one single person may oftentimes be broken, as it seemeth to himself, but the whole Body of Christ was never broken, nor never shall be, without end. And therefore a sure thing it is, a good and a gracious, to will meekly and mightily to be fastened and **oned** to our Mother, Holy Church, that is, Christ Jesus. For the food of mercy is His dearworthy blood and precious water is plenteous to make us fair and clean; the blessed wounds of our Saviour be open and enjoy to heal us; the sweet, gracious hands of our Mother be ready and diligently about us. For He in all this working useth the office of a kind nurse that hath nought else to do but to give heed about the salvation of her child.

It is His office to save us: it is His worship to do [for] us, and it is His will [that] we know it: for He willeth that we love Him sweetly and trust in Him meekly and mightily. And this shewed He in these gracious words: *I keep thee full surely.*

Chapter LXII

For in that time He shewed our frailty and our fallings, our afflictings and our settings at nought, our despites and our outcastings, and all our woe so far forth as methought it might befall in this life. And therewith He

waxeth Verb meaning "grows."

adread Afraid.

lother Loathsome, loathing.

ruth From the verb *rewen*, to rue. Noun meaning compassion, pity, sympathy. Compare to antonym *ruthless*.

oned To be one with.

shewed His blessed Might, His blessed Wisdom, His blessed Love: that He keepeth us in this time as tenderly and as sweetly to His worship, and as surely to our salvation, as He doeth when we are in most solace and comfort. And thereto He raiseth us spiritually and highly in heaven, and turneth it all to His worship and to our joy, without end. For His love suffereth us never to lose time.

And all this is of the Nature-Goodness of God, by the working of Grace. God is Nature[5] in His being: that is to say, that Goodness that is Nature, it is God. He is the ground, He is the substance, He is the same thing that is Nature-hood.[6] And He is very Father and very Mother of Nature: and all natures that He hath made to flow out of Him to work His will shall be restored and brought again into Him by the salvation of man through the working of Grace.

For of all natures[7] that He hath set in diverse creatures by part, in man is all the whole; in fullness and in virtue, in fairness and in goodness, in royalty and nobleness, in all manner of majesty, of preciousness and worship. Here may we see that we are all beholden to God for nature, and we are all beholden to God for grace. Here may we see us

> 66 *Thus in [our] Very Mother, Jesus, our life is grounded, in the foreseeing Wisdom of Himself from without beginning, with the high Might of the Father, the high sovereign Goodness of the Holy Ghost.* 99

needeth not greatly to seek far out to know sundry natures, but to Holy Church, unto our Mother's breast: that is to say, unto our own soul where our Lord dwelleth; and there shall we find all now in faith and in understanding. And afterward verily in Himself clearly, in bliss.

But let no man nor woman take this singularly to himself: for it is not so, it is general: for it is [of] our precious Christ, and to Him was this fair nature adight[8] for the worship and nobility of man's making, and for the joy and the bless of man's salvation; even as He saw, wist, and knew from without beginning.

Chapter LXIII

Here may we see that we have verily of Nature to hate sin, and we have verily of Grace to hate sin. For Nature is all good and fair in itself, and Grace was sent out to save Nature and destroy sin, and bring again fair nature to the blessed point from whence it came: that is God; with more nobleness and worship by the virtuous working of Grace. For it shall be seen afore God by all His Holy in joy without end that Nature has been assayed in the fire of tribulation and therein hath been found no flaw, no fault.[9] Thus are Nature and Grace of one accord: For Grace is God, as Nature is God: He is two in manner of working and one in love; and neither of these worketh without other: they be not disparted.

And when we by Mercy of God and with His help accord us to Nature and Grace, we shall see verily that sin is in sooth viler and more painful than hell, without likeness: for it is contrary to our fair nature. For as verily as sin is unclean, so verily is it unnatural,[10] and thus an horrible thing to see for the loved soul that would be all fair and shining in the sight of God, as Nature and Grace teacheth.

Yet be we not adread of this, save inasmuch as dread may speed us: but meekly make we our moan to our dearworthy Mother, and He shall besprinkle us in His precious blood and make our soul full soft and full mild, and heal us full fair by process of time, right as it is most worship to Him and joy to us without end. And of this sweet fair working He shall never cease nor stint till all His dearworthy children be born and forth-brought. (And that shewed He where He shewed [me] understanding of the **ghostly** Thirst, that is the love-longing that shall last till **Doomsday**.)

Thus in [our] Very Mother, Jesus, our life is grounded, in the foreseeing Wisdom of Himself from without beginning, with the high Might of the Father, the high sovereign Goodness of the Holy Ghost. And in the taking of our nature He **quickened** us; in His blessed dying upon the Cross He bare us to endless life; and from that time, and now, and evermore unto Doomsday, He feedeth us and

ghostly Spiritual.

Doomsday The day of the final judgment at the end of the world.

quickened Made alive, brought to life, stimulated.

furthereth us: even as that high sovereign Kindness of Motherhood, and as Kindly need of Childhood asketh. . . .

And I understood none higher stature in this life than Childhood, in feebleness and failing of might and of wit, unto the time that our Gracious Mother hath brought us up to our Father's bliss. And then shall it verily be known to us His meaning in those sweet words where He saith: *And all shall be well: and thou shalt see, thyself, that all manner of things shall be well.* And then shall the Bliss of our Mother, in Christ, be new to begin in the Joys of our God: which new beginning shall last without end, new beginning.

Thus I understand that all His blessed children which be come out of Him by Nature shall be brought again into Him by Grace.

Endnotes

1. "I it am."
2. "so kynd of the self."
3. "kynde," "kind."
4. "bristinid."
5. "kynde."
6. "kindhede."
7. "kyndes."
8. i.e. made ready, prepared, appointed.
9. "no lak (blame), no defaute."
10. "as sothly as sin is onclene as sothly is it onkinde."

For Reflection

1. What is the significance of describing Christ as "It is I" or, in Julian's original English, "I it am"? Find the "I am" sayings of Jesus in the Gospel of John (I am the light, I am the good shepherd, etc.) and use them to support your answer.

2. How does Julian describe the Church? How does she see the Church in relationship to Christ?

3. How would you describe God's "Fatherhood and Motherhood"?

4. Why does Julian exhort us to "use the condition of a child" when relating to "our heavenly Mother, Jesus"?

Part 3
Marks of the Church

12 "A Tower of Refuge": Overview of the Marks of the Church

Introduction

Saint Thomas Aquinas (1225–1274), one of the greatest philosophers and theologians of the Middle Ages, was born near Naples, Italy, and entered the **Dominican Order** as a young man while studying at the University of Paris. Upon completing his studies, which took him to Cologne, Germany, to study with Saint Albert the Great (Albertus Magnus), he began a teaching career in Italy and at the University of Paris. He is best known for his *Summa Contra Gentiles*, said to have been written for use by Dominican missionaries, and the exhaustive *Summa Theologiae*, which sets out a systematic understanding of the fundamental truths of Church teaching concerning God and creation; the nature of the human being in terms of free will, grace, and morality; and Jesus Christ as the mediator between God and humanity. Aquinas employed the categories of **Aristotelian metaphysics** because at the time, they were the language of philosophy and science, and the *quaestio disputata* method of investigation. The writing, therefore, is direct and practical, arguing methodically from sensory data, as a scientific method might do. By analyzing the "data" concerning God, humanity, and Christ, Aquinas recognized that the key issue involved reason and revelation. Human beings are capable of attaining certain kinds of truth through the application of human reason, but other truths need to

> ### *Quaestio Disputata*
>
> Popular in the Middle Ages, this was a form of study and debate in which a question is posed, a position taken, the position supported, and then a counterargument presented for the same position, with supporting evidence. This process was repeated until the correct answer, or truth, emerged.

be revealed through God's grace or Divine Revelation (see chapter 7, "The Church as Mystery").

Aquinas wrote this chapter's selection, "I Believe in the Holy Catholic Church," not as a theological treatise but as a homily, given during Lent in 1273. In it he presents an overview of all four marks of the Church: One, Holy, Catholic, and Apostolic.

Dominican Order The Dominican Order is the popular name for the religious order known as the Order of Preachers (Ordo Praedicatorum), dedicated to preaching, teaching, and study. The order was founded by Saint Dominic (1170–1221) at Bologna, Italy, in 1220.

Aristotelian metaphysics A science of being that connected ideas with physical objects and used categories such as form, matter, essence, and cause to describe the physical universe. Aquinas applied these categories to the invisible world of faith and revelation.

He focuses on a theme of this primary source reader on the Church: the Church is the Body of Christ, who is her Head. Aquinas discusses the four marks of the Church in light of this Body, which is neither male nor female and is distinct from other churches and organizations. Note that the four marks of the Church are named in the Nicene Creed, proclaimed at the conclusion of the Liturgy of the Word at each Mass.

The marks of the Church are vital to the Church's identity, not because they describe the Church from the outside, "what it looks like," but because these marks characterize and define the inner life of the Church as it springs from her soul, the Holy Spirit. The Marks of the Church, seen outwardly, flow from the Church's innermost reality.

It is interesting to note that Aquinas acknowledges a preliminary condition of the Church before speaking about these marks. The Church, he says, is an *ecclesia*, which means the people must gather, come together, assemble in a holy place for a holy purpose: to give glory and honor to God. Once they do this, the world will see that the Church truly is One, Holy, Catholic, and Apostolic. But it is only through the blood of Christ and the anointing of the Holy Spirit that this becomes possible.

Excerpt from *Exposition on the Apostles' Creed*

By Saint Thomas Aquinas

NINTH ARTICLE

I BELIEVE IN THE HOLY CATHOLIC CHURCH

As in one man there is one soul and one body, yet many members withal: even so the Catholic Church is one body, having many members. The soul that quickens this body is the Holy Ghost: and therefore after confessing our belief in the Holy Ghost, we are bid to believe in the Holy Catholic Church: hence the Creed continues—*The Holy Catholic Church.*

Here be it observed that the word *Ecclesia* (Church) signifies assembly: wherefore the Holy Church signifies the assembly of the faithful, and the individual Christian is as a member of the Church, of which it is said (Ecclus. li, 23): *Draw near to me, ye unlearned, and gather yourselves together into the house of discipline.* This Holy Church has four conditions in that she is one, holy, catholic, i.e. universal, and strong, i.e. firmly established.

(1) With regard to the first, it must be noted that although various heretics have formed themselves into various sects, they do not belong to the Church, since they are so many divisions, whereas the Church is one: *One is my dove: my perfect one is but one* (Cant. vi, 8). The unity of the Church arises from three sources.—Firstly, from the unity of faith, in as much as all Christians who belong to the body of the Church have the same belief: *I beseech you . . . that you all speak the same thing: and that there be no schisms among you* (I Cor. i, 10). *One God, one faith, one baptism* (Eph. iv, 10).—Secondly, from the unity of hope, since all are confirmed in the hope of obtaining eternal life:

> " *The unity of the Church arises from three sources.—Firstly, from the unity of faith, in as much as all Christians who belong to the body of the Church have the same belief. . . . Secondly, from the unity of hope, since all are confirmed in the hope of obtaining eternal life. . . . Thirdly, from the unity of charity, in as much as all are united in loving God, and bound to one another in mutual love. . . .* "

wherefore the Apostle says (Eph. iv, 4): *One body, and one Spirit: as you are called in one hope of your calling.*—Thirdly, from the unity of charity, in as much as all are united in loving God, and bound to one another in mutual love: *The glory which thou hast given me, I have given to them: that they may be one as we also are one* (John xvii, 22). If this love is true it is evinced in the mutual solicitude and sympathy of the members: *That we may in all things grow up in him who is the head, even Christ: from whom the whole body being compacted and fitly joined together, by what every joint supplieth, according to the operation in the measure of every part, maketh increase of the body, unto the edifying of itself in charity* (Eph. iv, 15, 16), because each one ought to be of service to his neighbour by making use of the grace that God has bestowed upon him. Therefore no man should think it of small account or allow himself to be cut off and expelled from this Church: for there is but one Church wherein men find salvation, even as outside the Ark of Noe it was not possible for anyone to be saved.

(2) With regard to the second, be it observed that there is also another assembly, that of the wicked: *I have hated the assembly of the malignant* (Ps. xxv, 5). But this is an evil assembly, whereas Christ's Church is holy: *The temple of God is holy, which ye are* (I Cor. iii, 17); hence the words, *The holy . . . Church.* In this Church the faithful are sanctified by four things.

(*a*) In the first place, just as when a church is consecrated, it is cleansed materially, even so the faithful are washed with the blood of Christ: *He hath loved us and washed us* from our sins; in his own blood (Apoc. i, 5). *Jesus, that he might sanctify the people by his own blood, suffered outside the gate* (Heb. xiii, 12).

(*b*) Secondly, they are sanctified by being anointed because, just as a church is anointed, so also are the faithful anointed with a spiritual **unction** unto sanctification; otherwise they would not be Christians, since Christ is the same as Anointed. This unction is the grace of the Holy Ghost: *God who hath*

> **unction** From the Latin *unguere*, "to anoint," an unction is an ointment used in anointing, for healing, or for consecration. Aquinas explains that the spiritual unction of Christians is the grace of the Holy Spirit.

anointed us (2 Cor. ii, 21). *Ye are sanctified . . . in the name of our Lord Jesus* (I Cor. vi, 11).

(*c*) Thirdly, by the indwelling Trinity, since wheresoever God dwells, that place is holy: Verify, this place is holy (Gen. xxviii, 16). *Holiness becometh thy house, 0 Lord* (Ps. xcii, 5).

(*d*) Fourthly, because God is invoked over them: *But thou, O Lord, art among us, and thy name hath been called upon us* (Jer. xiv, 9).

We must, therefore, beware, seeing that we are thus sanctified, lest by sin we defile our soul which is God's temple: *If any man violate the temple of God, him shall God destroy* (I Cor. iii, 17).

(3) With regard to the third, we must observe that the Church is catholic or universal—firstly, in point of place, in that it is spread throughout the whole world, contrary to the teaching of the **Donatists**: *Your faith is spoken of in the whole world* (Rom. i, 8). *Go ye into the whole world and preach the gospel to every creature* (Mark xvi, 15). Formerly, God was known only in Judea, whereas now He is known throughout the whole world. In this sense the Church has three parts: one is on earth, another in Heaven, the third is in Purgatory.—Secondly, the Church is universal as regards the different conditions of humanity, in as much as no exceptions are made, for it includes master and servant, male and female: *There is neither male nor female* (Gal. iii, 18).— Thirdly, it is universal in point of time. For there have been those who said that the Church was to last until a certain time; but this is false, since this Church began from the time of Abel and will endure to the end of the world: *Behold, I am with you all days, even to the consummation of the world* (Matt. xxviii, 20), and after the end of the world it will continue in Heaven.

(4) The fourth condition is that the Church is firmly estab-

Donatists

The Donatists were followers of Donatus, a bishop in fourth-century North Africa. He taught, heretically, that the effectiveness of a Sacrament depended upon the moral character of the person who administered it. On the contrary, God's grace is not dependent on the moral quality of the minister. Donatists were criticized for their concern only for their own small area of North Africa, rather than for the universal Church.

lished. A house is said to be firmly established when (*a*) it has good foundations. Now the Church's chief foundation is Christ: *Other foundation no man can lay but that which is laid, which is Christ Jesus* (I Cor. iii, 11). The Apostles and their doctrine are the Church's secondary foundation, whence she derives her stability which is described (Apoc. xxi, 14) where it is said that the city had *twelve foundations, wherein were* inscribed *the names of the twelve apostles.* Hence the Church is called Apostolic. Moreover, it was to indicate the stability of the Church that the Blessed Peter is called the *head.*

(*b*) Secondly, a house is proved to be firmly built, if however much it be shaken, it remains standing; and the Church has ever proved indestructible. Her persecutors have failed to destroy her; in fact, it was during times of persecution that the Church grew more and more; the persecutors themselves, and those whom the Church would destroy, these it was who came to naught: *Whosoever shall fall on this stone shall be broken; but on whomsoever it shall fall, it shall grind to powder* (Matt. xxi, 44).—Again, errors have assailed her; in fact, the greater the number of errors that have arisen, the more has the truth been made manifest: *Men corrupt in mind, reprobate in faith: but they shall proceed no further* (2 Tim. iii, 8).—Nor has the Church failed before the assaults of demons: for she is like a tower of refuge to all who fight against the devil: *The name of the Lord is a strong tower* (Prov. xviii, 10). Hence the devil does his utmost to destroy the Church: but he prevails not, for our Lord said (Matt. xvi, 18) *that the gates of hell shall not prevail against it,* as though to say: "They will war against thee, but they shall not overcome thee." The result is that alone the Church of Peter (to whom it befell to evangelize Italy when the disciples were sent to preach) was always strong in faith; and whereas outside that Church there is either no faith at all, or it is mingled with many errors, nevertheless the Church of Peter flourishes in faith and is immune from error. Nor need we wonder at this, since the Lord said to Peter (Luke xxii, 32): *I have prayed for thee, Peter, that thy faith may not fail.*

For Reflection

1. How do you see the Church living the reality of being One, Holy, Catholic, and Apostolic? What are obstacles to fully realizing these characteristics in the life of the Church?

2. What does it mean to be one "*as we also are one* (John xvii, 22)"? Is such unity possible?

3. How is the Church "a tower of refuge" for the faithful today? What do you see as the greatest challenges facing the Church today?

4. Which of the marks of the Church could you most easily explain if questioned or challenged?

13 First Mark: The Church Is One

Introduction

As we saw in chapter 1, the early Church was composed of people from throughout the Roman Empire ("We are Parthians, Medes, and Elamites, inhabitants of Mesopotamia, Judea and Cappadocia, Pontus and Asia, Phrygia and Pamphylia, Egypt and the districts of Libya near Cyrene, as well as travelers from Rome" [Acts of the Apostles 2:9–10]). Yet the story of the Church is one of unity, and, as Berard Marthaler (b. 1927) explains in this chapter's reading, the Church became one even though it was made up of people from many places. In fact, unity was a major theme as the Church continued to grow throughout the world. One might ask today, How is it possible for a Nigerian, American, Argentine, and Pole to claim membership in the same institution, all incorporated into the Roman Catholic Church? Perhaps the answer lies in the word *incorporate*, which comes from Latin and means "to become enfleshed in one body." Thus the metaphor developed in the early Church and used extensively by Saint Paul and others is the Body of Christ (see Ephesians 1:15–23). Becoming one with Christ means becoming one with one another in his Body or the community known as Church. How is this achieved? We hear it in the words of the liturgy and in our Trinitarian theology: through God's grace acting in the name of Christ through the power of the Holy Spirit.

Through the same power of the Holy Spirit, another miracle occurs. The unity that comes out of diversity does not wipe diversity away. It enhances it by allowing Nigerians, Americans, Argentines, and Poles to share who and what they are with one another, thereby creating greater self-understanding and identity. It's as simple as this: the more we know about other people and their cultures, hopefully the more we become curious about our own culture and the richness of our cultural heritage. As we learn about one another and ourselves, we bring such depth of knowledge and love to worship, which, in turn, leads us to share more and to take Christ's message of salvation out to the world. This is a fundamental paradox of the Holy Spirit working through the Church: the more we share with one another, the more we receive. This may require us to risk sharing ourselves and adapting our preferred way of doing things, but Christ requires no less, for salvation has been offered to everyone (see Romans 1:16–17). Thus, the author particularly emphasizes the unity of the Church in this excerpt, noting that this is both a gift of the Holy Spirit and a challenging task for all members of the Body of Christ.

Finally, Father Marthaler, a Franciscan priest, Church historian, and former professor at the Catholic University of America, in Washington, D.C., reminds us that the universal Church is called to be one, and so the last part of the reading is a brief summary of the modern ecumenical movement, which includes all Christian Churches and faith communities: Roman Catholic, Orthodox, and Protestant. As Pope Saint John Paul II stated in the encyclical *Ut Unum Sint* (1995), the Christian Church is in the world "to announce and witness, to make present and spread the mystery of communion which is essential to her, and to gather all people and all things into Christ, so as to be for all an 'inseparable sacrament of unity'" (5).

Excerpt from *The Creed: The Apostolic Faith in Contemporary Theology*
By Berard Marthaler

The Marks of the Church

"One holy catholic and apostolic"

To say as we did in the previous chapter that the early church did not develop a systematic ecclesiology does not mean that Christians made no effort to set forth an organized understanding of the church. Given the number of groups—various gnostic schools, the **Marcionites**, the **Montanists**, and more obscure sects—catechumens as well as the faithful needed guidance in judging who represented the authentic gospel message. St. Cyprian complains about people who "still call themselves Christians after abandoning the Gospel of Christ and the observance of his law."[1] In the face of the confusion caused from without by rival claimants and from within by factionalism and schism, the church argued its case on the basis of its unity, holiness, universality, and apostolicity. These essential characteristics that distinguish the true church from other groups have come to be known as "notes" or "marks" of the church. They served as a basis for catechesis and gave rise to a kind of rule-of-thumb expressed in the Creed of Constantinople as WE BELIEVE IN ONE HOLY CATHOLIC AND APOSTOLIC CHURCH.

In this chapter we examine the implications of the four marks of the church. Our theme is that unity, holiness, catholicity, and apostolicity are not only endowments given to the church by the Holy Spirit but also tasks that challenge the church at every level, from the church universal to the church that is the Archdiocese of Chicago to the Church of the Holy Trinity in Norfolk, Virginia, and the cathedral parish in Toronto, Ontario. Thus we survey the efforts of the modern ecumenical movement to make the unity of the church manifest in a divided world. In connection with apostolicity we discuss the special role of the Apostle Peter and **Petrine office** that was once the focus of church unity but is now an obstacle for many.

Marcionites Followers of the second-century heretic Marcion, who taught that grace was all one needed for salvation, not the Law (i.e., the Ten Commandments). He rejected the Scriptures of the Old Testament, as well as certain Gospels. His Christology downplayed the humanity and sufferings of Christ.

Montanists Followers of Montanus, a second-century leader of an apocalyptic movement, who announced the end of the world and the establishment of God's kingdom in Phrygia (modern Turkey, not far from the Black Sea).

Petrine Office The Office of Peter, or the specific ministry of the Pope, which differs from other ministries and involves governance in conjunction with fellow bishops.

Before we deal directly with the marks of the church, however, we must make a distinction. . . . Both the Nicene and Apostles' Creeds affirm belief in the church: the briefer form of the latter states WE BELIEVE IN THE HOLY CATHOLIC CHURCH; the longer form of the Nicene Creed adds ONE and APOSTOLIC. The church is indeed an object of faith, but not in the same way that God is the object of faith. In commenting on this phrase, medieval theologians carefully explained that we believe in the Holy Spirit, not only *in se* ["in himself"], but as the one who makes the church one, holy, catholic, and apostolic.[2] The existence of the church in itself is not a matter of faith. Historians and sociologists of all religious traditions and no religious tradition accept the church as a social group made up of people who profess to be Christians. But the church as mystery eludes reason and is beyond empirical study; because of its origins, nature, and destiny the church demands faith. The Catechism of the Council of Trent, commenting on the Apostles' Creed, stated it in this way:

> But with regard to the three Persons of the Trinity, the Father, the Son and the Holy Spirit, we believe in such a way that we place our faith in them. Here, however, the form of speech is changed and we profess to believe "the Holy Catholic Church," and not *in* the Holy Catholic Church. This difference of expression distinguishes God, the author of all things, from created things and refers to the divine goodness all these exalted benefits which are gathered together for us in the Church.[3]

ONE AND UNDIVIDED

In the first article of the creed we confess belief in *one* God by way of taking a stance against polytheism and idolatry; the unicity of God implies a unity within the Godhead, but the emphasis is on the uniqueness of God. In the third article we confess ONE CHURCH, but the emphasis here is on unity and only secondarily on the church's uniqueness. Unity implies both oneness and diversity: the church is one in that it presents a certain integrity or wholeness (which, we shall see below, means "catholic"). On the other hand, as St. Paul recognized in using the image of the body and its members, the church is made up of individuals of various backgrounds and diverse gifts. Despite differences they are one in confessing that Jesus Christ is Lord and in looking to him as their Savior. Nothing in the New Testament suggests that uniformity—the denial of diversity—is an ideal, and the history of the church is evidence that it has never been a reality.[4]

Unity in the Holy Spirit does not mean imposing on the church's life and thought a uniform pattern that ignores individual charisms and personal talents. Congar cites Jesus'

> **Council of Trent**
>
> Convened by Pope Paul III, this Council took place over the extended period of 1545 to 1563. It was interrupted by war and the threat of disease. This council covered both dogma and Church discipline and dealt with issues brought up by the Protestant Reformation. It formally established the number of Sacraments at seven and produced the *Roman Missal* and the *Roman Catechism*, both of which were in use well into the twentieth century.

allegory of the Good Shepherd, pointing out that while the church may be compared to the sheepfold or enclosure, the flock is made up of individual sheep, each of which the shepherd calls by name (Jn 10:1–3, 16). In a passage that is doubly sad because it sounds autobiographical, Yves Congar laments the Catholic church's excessive reliance on authority to maintain unity. In the modern era there has been a tendency to confuse unity and uniformity, to reduce order to observance of imposed rules. It has led, he writes, "to the development of a system of supervision that has been effective in maintaining an orthodox line and framework, but this has been achieved at the price of marginalizing individuals who have had something to say, and often even reducing them to silence and inactivity."*

No less a power than the Spirit of God is necessary to bring the many diverse peoples and individuals who make up the church to a sense of solidarity, "It was in one Spirit that all of us, whether Jew or Greek, slave or free, were baptized into one body. All of us have been given to drink

---

*In February 1954, Congar was forbidden to teach. In 1956 he was given a limited assignment in Strasbourg. Despite suspicion and adversity, however, Congar continued to research and write. The concluding sentence to the paragraph quoted above reads: "Sometimes those persons have said what they have to say, but they have usually done so in irregular and unfavorable conditions." *Lumen Gentium*, the *Constitution on the Church*, promulgated by Vatican II, incorporates many of Congar's insights and stands as a vindication of his lifelong efforts. In 1994 Pope Saint John Paul II named him to the College of Cardinals. He died in Paris June 22, 1995.

of the one Spirit" (1 Cor 12:13). It is important to keep in mind that the Holy Spirit is not the Spirit of the church but the Spirit of God, so that it is one and the same Uncreated Spirit who is both in the head, Christ, and in his body, the church. In essence, unity in the Spirit is always communion—"union with." The Western church has traditionally ascribed to the Holy Spirit a unitive function within the Trinity, the bonding of Father and Son in love; similarly, the mission of the Holy Spirit in the world is seen as uniting believers to one another and to God in the Body of Christ. The Spirit, the principle of unity in the church, is also the source of the love that the members have for one another in their hearts.[5] Jesus prayed to his heavenly Father that his disciples "may be one, even as we are one" (Jn 17:11). Ideally the church is called to mirror the tri-unity of God, the indivisible unity that binds Father, Son, and Spirit and at the same time acknowledges the distinctive properties of each. In describing the unity of the church, St. Cyprian uses the same language that Tertullian used in describing the Trinity: And the Church forms a unity, of which each holds his part in its totality. And the Church forms a unity, however far she spreads and multiplies by the progeny of her fecundity; just as the sun's rays are many, yet the light is one, and a tree's branches are many, the strength deriving from its sturdy root is one. So too, though many streams flow from a single spring, though its multiplicity seems scattered abroad by the copiousness of its welling waters, yet their oneness abides by reason of their starting point.[6]

The paragraph in *Lumen gentium* that sets forth the special role of the Holy Spirit ends with another quotation from St. Cyprian to the effect that the church shines forth as "a people made one with the unity of the Father, the Son, and the Holy Spirit" (para. 4).[7]

The Ecumenical Movement One of the chief concerns of the Second Vatican Council . . . was to promote the restoration of unity among all Christians. The Decree on Ecumenism was emphatic in stating that without doubt a divided Christendom "openly contradicts the will of Christ, provides a stumbling block to the world, and inflicts damage on the most holy cause of proclaiming the good news to every creature" (para. 1). "Ecumenism" is a relatively new word to describe efforts to bring the churches into communion with one another, but ecumenism is not new. In medieval times

> ❝ *The mission of the Holy Spirit in the world is seen as uniting believers to one another and to God in the Body of Christ. The Spirit, the principle of unity in the church, is also the source of the love that the members have for one another in their hearts.* ❞

repeated attempts were made to heal the breach between Eastern and Western churches, notably at the Councils of Lyons (1274) and Florence (1438–1439); in the early stages of the Protestant Reformation **irenic**-minded leaders made concerted efforts to mend differences and thereby forestall a breakup of Western Christendom. Over the years sporadic moves, especially among Protestants, continued to be made to negotiate working agreements and, thereby, to establish some semblance of unity and cooperation among the various Christian bodies.

The modern ecumenical movement dates, for most practical purposes, from the Edinburgh Missionary Conference in 1910. Representatives of mission boards and mission societies of many Protestant bodies came together to study their endeavors, especially in non-Christian lands, with an eye to making the work of evangelization more effective. A principal obstacle to effective evangelization, recognized by all, was the scandal caused by Christians being divided among themselves and competing with one another. The conference presented a vision of world Christianity and created a climate for greater cooperation among the churches. It was the forerunner of the Life and Work Conference that met for the first time in Stockholm in 1925. Dedicated to involving the churches in social, economic, and political issues, it formulated the slogan, "Doctrine divides, service unites," because it seemed easier to get the churches to work together on practical problems than

irenic Favoring peace, moderation, or conciliation.

to agree on points of doctrine. The slogan had an element of truth, but it was also simplistic insofar as doctrinal issues were perceived to be unimportant or impractical. As a corrective, the first of the Faith and Order Conferences met in Lausanne (Switzerland) in 1927 to address theological and ecclesiastical questions with an eye to unity in faith and church structure.

Endnotes

1. *Unity of the Church*, ch. 3; ACW, p. 45.
2. Yves Congar, *I Believe in the Holy Spirit* (New York: Seabury Press, 1983), II, pp. 6–7. Henri de Lubac, *La Foi chretienne*, chs. 4–6. J. P. L. Oulton, "The Apostles' Creed and Belief Concerning the Church," *Journal of Theological Studies* 39 (1938): 239–243.
3. Article 9, n. 22. Bradley and Kevane, p. 111.
4. Yves Congar, *Diversity and Communion* (Mystic, CT: Twenty-Third Publications, 1985), pp. 9–43.
5. Congar, *I Believe*, I, p. 119.
6. Cyprian, *Unity of the Church*, ch. 5. ACW, no. 25, pp. 47–48.
7. The quotation is from Cyprian's treatise *On the Lord's Prayer*, 23. Congar calls attention to this passage, saying that this text from Cyprian inspired him in writing *Divided Christendom*. One also suspects that Congar in turn inspired the passage in *Lumen Gentium*, par. 4.

For Reflection

1. What do you think Marthaler means when he says that the marks of the Church are not only endowments or gifts to the Church but also tasks to be done at every level?

2. Discuss the relationship between unity and diversity in terms of mystery as presented so far in this text. How are they related?

3. What do you suppose are some of the practical obstacles to achieving unity in your parish, school, or diocese? How might they be overcome? What efforts have already been made toward unity?

4. Describe any local ecumenical efforts undertaken by your parish and other faith communities in your area. How can you contribute to ecumenical efforts?

14 Second Mark: The Church Is Holy

Introduction

In the introduction to the Rite of Penance, prepared by the Congregation for Divine Worship and approved by Pope Paul VI in 1973, is a reference to Ephesians 5:25–26, which states that Christ "loved the Church and gave himself up for it to make it holy" (II, 3). This appears in the Rite of Penance, because, as implausible as it may sound, holiness is related to sin. Holiness, whether for an individual Christian or the universal Church, does not require perfection. In fact, it is just the opposite. What makes us holy is an unvarnished recognition of who and what we are—our sins—and the willingness to repent of them and follow Christ. Holiness, therefore, is not a static end point to reach or a finish line to cross but rather a constant struggle with selfishness and whatever tendencies we may have to withdraw from others, either by design or disposition. Sin is hiding our true selves, which is what Adam and Eve did after rebelling against God.

> *The Church, having sinners in its midst, is at the same time holy and in need of cleansing, and so is unceasingly intent on repentance and reform.*

Saint Augustine spoke of this struggle as taking place between two kingdoms: the Reign of God and the reign of Satan, or, put another way, between love of God and love of self. Interestingly, the German adult catechism refers to this struggle as the "signature" characteristic of humanity.[1]

As you read this chapter's excerpt, you will see that, quoting *Lumen Gentium*, it acknowledges the struggle within the community, as well as the individual: "The Church, having sinners in its midst, is at the same time holy and in need of cleansing, and so is unceasingly intent on repentance and reform" (II, 3). This is an amazing recognition of the human condition and how that condition exists in and is expressed through the Body of Christ, the Church. Yet it is precisely the Church that is the meeting place for the encounter between the human and divine and the channel through which the grace of Christ flows for salvation. This is holiness, which is achieved not just on the individual level but also the communal one. As members of the Body of Christ, our holiness influences the entire Body, as does our sin. "The Church," as described in this excerpt, is not an abstraction but a living body, sharing both the wounds and the joy of all of its members.

The rite notes that "people frequently join together to commit injustice. But it is also true that they help each other in doing penance; freed from sin by the grace of Christ, they become, with all persons of good will, agents of justice and peace in the world" (II, 5). So the holiness that the Church claims (including the holiness of each member) is a real one, tested in the world and tempered by the repentance of sin and commitment to a new life that has already been won for us through the blood of Christ.

Excerpt from *The Rite of Penance* (Introduction)

From *The Rites of the Catholic Church*

INTRODUCTION

I. MYSTERY OF RECONCILIATION IN THE HISTORY OF SALVATION

1. The Father has shown forth his mercy by reconciling the world to himself in Christ and by making peace for all things on earth and in heaven by the blood of Christ on the cross. (See 2 Corinthians 5:18ff.; Colossians 1:20.) The Son of God made man lived among us in order to free us from the slavery of sin (see John 8:34–36) and to call us out of darkness into his wonderful light. (See 1 Peter 2:9.) He therefore began his work on earth

by preaching repentance and saying: "Repent and believe the Gospel" (Mark 1:15).

This invitation to repentance, which had often been sounded by the prophets, prepared people's hearts for the coming of the kingdom of God through the voice of John the Baptist, who came "preaching a baptism of repentance for the forgiveness of sins" (Mark 1:4).

Jesus, however, not only exhorted people to repentance so that they would abandon their sins and turn wholeheartedly to the Lord, (see Luke 15) but welcoming sinners, he actually reconciled them with the Father (Luke 5:20 and 27–32; 7:48). Moreover, he healed the sick in order to offer a sign of his power to forgive sin. (See Matthew 9:2–8.) Finally, he himself died for our sins and rose again for our justification. (See Romans 4:25.) Therefore, on the night he was betrayed and began his saving passion,[1] he instituted the sacrifice of the New Covenant in his blood for the forgiveness of sins. (See Matthew 26:28.) After his resurrection he sent the Holy Spirit upon the apostles, em-

Justification

The word *justification* is a theological concept describing a person's being made "righteous," or worthy of salvation, before God. (See also the definition in chapter 7 of this book.) Protestants and Roman Catholics have disagreed over the degree to which Christians cooperate in their own justification and how justification is given by Christ. The Catholic interpretation has emphasized the grace given by God to lead a Christian life after Baptism. Protestants generally have emphasized the necessity of faith. See Romans 3:21–31; 8:29–30.

Joint Declaration on the Doctrine of Justification

In 1998 the "Joint Declaration on the Doctrine of Justification" was signed between the Lutheran World Federation and the Catholic Church. This declaration explored the meaning of justification and declared: "We confess together that persons are justified by faith in the gospel 'apart from works prescribed by the law' (Romans 3:28)" (31). This document thus clarified the disagreement between Catholic and Protestant understandings of justification: We are not saved by good works but by faith. Good works are in themselves gifts of grace.

powering them to forgive or retain sins (see John 20:19–23) and sending them forth to all peoples to preach repentance and the forgiveness of sins in his name. (See Luke 24:47.)

The Lord said to Peter: "I will give you the keys of the kingdom of heaven, and whatever you bind on earth will be bound in heaven, and whatever you loose on earth will be loosed also in heaven" (Matthew 16:19). In obedience to this command, on the day of Pentecost Peter preached the forgiveness of sins by baptism: "Repent and let everyone of you be baptized in the name of Jesus Christ for the remission of sins" (Acts 2:38). (See Acts 3:19 and 26:17–30.) Since then the Church has never failed to call people from sin to conversion and through the celebration of penance to show the victory of Christ over sin.

2. This victory is first brought to light in baptism where our fallen nature is crucified with Christ so that the body of sin may be destroyed and we may no longer be slaves to sin, but rise with Christ and live for God. (See Romans 6:4–10.) For this reason the Church proclaims its faith in "one baptism for the forgiveness of sins."

In the sacrifice of the Mass the passion of Christ is again made present; his body given for us and his blood shed for the forgiveness of sins are offered to God again by the Church for the salvation of the world. For in the eucharist Christ is present and is offered as "the sacrifice which has made our peace"[2] with God and in order that "we may be brought together in unity"[3] by his Holy Spirit.

Furthermore, our Savior Jesus Christ, when he gave to his apostles and their successors power to forgive sins, instituted in his Church the sacrament of penance. Its purpose is that the faithful who fall into sin after baptism may be reconciled with God through the restoration of grace.[4] The Church "possesses both water and tears: the water of baptism, the tears of penance."[5]

II. RECONCILIATION OF PENITENTS IN THE CHURCH'S LIFE

THE CHURCH BOTH HOLY AND ALWAYS IN NEED OF PURIFICATION

3. Christ "loved the Church and gave himself up for it to make it holy" (Ephesians 5:25–26) and he united the Church to himself as a bride. (See Revelation 19:7.) He filled it with his divine gifts, (see Ephesians 1:22–23)

because it is his Body and his fullness; through the Church he spreads truth and grace upon all.

The members of the Church, however, are exposed to temptation and often fall into the wretchedness of sin. As a result, "whereas Christ, 'holy, harmless, undefiled' (Hebrews 7:26), knew no sin (see 2 Corinthians 5:21) but came solely to seek pardon for the sins of his people (see Hebrews 2:17), the Church, having sinners in its midst, is at the same time holy and in need of cleansing, and so is unceasingly intent on repentance and reform."[6]

PENANCE IN THE CHURCH'S LIFE AND LITURGY
4. The people of God accomplish and perfect this continual repentance in many different ways. They share in the sufferings of Christ (see 1 Peter 4:13) by enduring their own difficulties, carry out works of mercy and charity (see 1 Peter 4:8), and adopt ever more fully the outlook of the Gospel message. Thus the people of God become in the world a sign of conversion to God. All this the Church expresses in its life and celebrates in its liturgy when the faithful confess that they are sinners and ask pardon of God and of their brothers and sisters. This happens in penitential services, in the proclamation of the word of God, in prayer, and in the penitential parts of the eucharistic celebration.[7]

In the sacrament of penance the faithful "obtain from God's mercy pardon for having offended him and at the same time reconciliation with the Church, which they have wounded by their sins and which by charity, example, and prayer seeks their conversion."[8]

RECONCILIATION WITH GOD AND WITH THE CHURCH
5. Since every sin is an offense against God that disrupts our friendship with him, "the ultimate purpose of penance is that we should love God deeply and commit ourselves completely to him."[9] Therefore, the sinner who by the grace of a merciful God embraces the way of penance comes back to the Father who "first loved us"(1 John 4:19), to Christ who gave himself up for us (see Galatians 2:20; Ephesians 5:25), and to the Holy Spirit who has been poured out on us abundantly. (See Titus 3:6.)

"The hidden and gracious mystery of God unites us all through a supernatural bond: on this basis one person's sin harms the rest even as one person's goodness enriches them."[10] Penance always therefore entails reconciliation with our brethren and sisters who remain harmed by our sins.

In fact, people frequently join together to commit injustice. But it is also true that they help each other in doing penance; freed from sin by the grace of Christ, they become, with all persons of good will, agents of justice and peace in the world.

Endnotes

1. See *Roman Missal*, Eucharistic Prayer III. (Second Edition)
2. See *Roman Missal*, Eucharistic Prayer III. (Second Edition)
3. See *Roman Missal*, Eucharistic Prayer II. (Second Edition)
4. See Council of Trent, sess. 14, *De sacramento Paenitentiae*, chapter 1: Denz-Schön 1668 and 1670; can. 1: Denz-Schön 1701.
5. Ambrose, Ep. 41, 12; PL 16, 1116.
6. *LG* no. 8: *AAS* 57 (1965) 12; ConstDecrDecl 106.
7. See Council of Trent, sess. 14, *De sacramento Paenitentiae*: Denz-Schön 1638, 1740, 1743. SCR, Instr. EuchMyst, May 25, 1967, no. 35 [*DOL* 179, no. 1264]; *GIRM*, nos. 29, 30, 56 a, b, g [*DOL* 208, nos. 1419, 1420, 1446].
8. *LG* no. 11 [*DOL* 4, no. 141].
9. Paul VI, Ap. Canst. *Paenitemini*, Feb. 17, 1966: *AAS* 58 (1966) 179. See also *LG* no. 11 [*DOL* 4, no. 141].
10. Paul VI, Ap. Canst. *Indulgentiarum doctrina*, Jan. 1, 1967, no. 4 [*DOL* 386, no. 3158]. See also Pius XII, Encycl. *Mystici Corporis*, June 29, 1943: *AAS* 35 (1943) 213.

For Reflection

1. What role does the Sacrament of Penance and Reconciliation take in the life and holiness of the Church?

2. The Rite of Penance connects Penance with Baptism through the forgiveness of sins, regeneration of the spirit, and water: "The Church 'possesses both water and tears: the water of baptism, the tears of penance'" (I, 2). Does your experience of Penance support this connection? If not, discuss possible reasons.

3. You will notice that the Rite of Penance mentions "works of mercy" (II, 4) as evidence of repentance and conversion to God. As you think about the communities to which you belong (family, school, parish), how are they "at the same time holy and in need of cleansing" (II, 3)? How do you contribute to the holiness of these communities?

15 Third Mark: The Church Is Catholic

Introduction

Blessed John Henry Newman (1801–1890) was a theologian and priest in the Church of England, or the Anglican Church, at a time when there was much controversy over which Christian tradition held the truth of Christ and could legitimately call itself the visible or true Church. The First Vatican Council of the Roman Catholic Church (1869–1870) had proclaimed that the Pope held jurisdiction over the universal Church and that his teachings on faith and morals were infallible. It also reasserted the claim of the Council of Trent that *extra Ecclesiam nulla salus,* or outside the Roman Catholic Church there was no salvation. Keenly interested in these issues not just as a theologian but also as a person of faith, Newman identified two essential marks of the Church that he considered to be at the center of the controversy: apostolicity and catholicity. The first refers to Apostolic Succession and whether any church claiming to be the true Church teaches revealed truth as handed down by Christ to Peter and the Apostles. The second, catholicity, concerns whether the Church is composed of all people everywhere or is limited in scope to a certain geographic region, ethnic group, or linguistic family.

> **Papal Infallibility**
>
> Papal infallibility is a tradition formalized dogmatically at the First Vatican Council: when speaking on matters of faith or morals, the Pope is preserved from error by the grace of the Holy Spirit. Infallible pronouncements are part of the Church's teaching office (Magisterium), along with Ecumenical Councils like Vatican Council I and Vatican Council II. Infallible teachings must be in accord with the Church's Tradition and Holy Scripture.

schism A split or break. In reference to Christian Churches, a break in communion between two Christian traditions previously united (e.g., the Roman Catholic Church and the Reformation churches). Schism is distinct from heresy, which is the rejection of beliefs or dogma.

The conclusion that Newman eventually came to was that, although the Anglican Church could claim apostolicity—its teachings seemed more in accord with what he called the "Primitive Creed"—he nevertheless determined that because the Roman Catholic Church was universal and had a well-developed corpus of doctrine developed from the Primitive Creed, it was, in fact, the true Church: "I am very far more sure that England is in **schism** than that the Roman additions to the Primitive Creed may not be developments, arising out of a keen and vivid realizing of the Divine Depositum of Faith" (*Apologia Pro Vita Sua*). He wrote elsewhere that doctrine can develop over time as long as it is rooted in the original teaching, even if in an implicit way. Thus he was more concerned with a church that he deemed not universal than with one that had developed doctrine to meet the changing needs of the times.

Beatification

Beatification is the third of four phases in the canonization process. (A potential candidate for sainthood is first declared a Servant of God, then Venerable. The fourth phase is canonization as a saint.) Though not yet a declaration of sainthood, beatification is the Church's official recognition that a person has gone to Heaven and can intercede with God on behalf of the living. The person beatified is known as "Blessed."

Shortly upon resolving this issue, he left the Anglican Church and became a full member of the Roman Catholic Church, eventually becoming a cardinal. His theological writings and his dedication to the Church have continued to remain influential even after his death. His decision to enter the Church is regarded as a heroic example of the pursuit of truth, despite personal anguish. He was beatified in 2010 by Pope Benedict XVI.

The passage that follows is taken from the last in a series of pamphlets written by Newman on the Anglican Church's *Thirty-Nine Articles*, which defined the Anglican Church's basic theology. He was still an Anglican at the time but had serious doubts about his role and position in that Church. He presents Article XIX, commenting on its description of *church* but then criticizing its condemnation of the Roman Catholic Church. Several things to note are the many descriptions of the Church taken from the writings of theologians and saints through history; Newman's defense of Catholicism; the emphasis on Word and Sacrament in the visible Church; and the Holy Spirit's presence in the Church, empowering her to endure internal imperfection and external threats over the course of time. Finally, note Newman's caveat concerning his quotation of an Anglican homily for Pentecost (Whitsunday): He makes clear he is only quoting it to illustrate his previous points about the Church and is not affirming the homily's concluding remark critical of "the Church of Rome" (the Roman Catholic Church).

Excerpt from *Tracts for the Times: Remarks on Certain Passages in the Thirty-Nine Articles* (Tract 90)

By John Henry Newman

ß 4.—*The Visible Church.*

Art. xix.—"The visible Church of Christ is a congregation of faithful men (*cœtus fidelium*), in the which the pure Word of God is preached, and the Sacraments be duly ministered, according to Christ's ordinance, in all those things that of necessity are requisite to the same."

This is not an abstract definition of *a* Church, but a description of *the* actually existing One Holy Catholic Church diffused throughout the world; as if it were read, "The Church is a certain society of the faithful," &c. This is evident from the mode of describing the Catholic Church familiar to all writers from the first stages down to the age of this Article. For instance, St. Clement of Alexandria says, "I mean by the Church, not a place, but the *congregation of the elect*." Origen: "The Church, the *assembly of all the faithful*." St. Ambrose: "*One congregation*, one Church." St. Isidore: "The Church is a *congregation of saints*, collected on a certain faith, and the best conduct of life." St. Augustin: "The Church is *the people of God* through all ages." Again: "The Church is *the multitude* which is spread over the whole earth." St. Cyril: "When we speak of the Church, we denote the most holy *multitude of the pious*." Theodoret: "The Apostle calls the Church *the assembly of the faithful*." Pope Gregory: "The Church, a *multitude of the faithful* collected of both sexes." Bede: "The Church is the *congregation of all saints*." Alcuin: "The Holy Catholic Church,—in Latin, the *congregation of the faithful*." Amalarius: "The Church is *the people* called together by the Church's ministers." Pope Nicolas I: "The Church, that is, the *congregation of Catholics*." St. Bernard: "What is the Spouse, but *the congregation of the just*?" Peter the Venerable: "The Church is called *a congregation*, but not of all things, not of cattle, but of *men, faithful*, good, just. Though bad among these good, and just among the unjust, are revealed or concealed, yet it is called a Church." Hugo Victorinus: "The Holy Church, that is, *the university of the faithful*." Arnulphus: "The Church is called *the congregation of the faithful*." Albertus Magnus: "The Greek word Church means in Latin convocation; and whereas works and callings belong to rational animals, and reason in man is inward faith, therefore it is called *the congregation of the faithful*." Durandus: "The Church is in one sense material, in which divers offices are celebrated; in another spiritual, which is the *collection of the faithful*." Alvarus: "The Church is *the multitude of the faithful*, or the university of Christians." Pope Pius II: "The Church is *the multitude of the faithful* dispersed through all nations."

[And so the Reformers, in their own way, for instance, the Confession of Augsburgh. "The one Holy Church will remain for ever. Now the Church of Christ properly is the congregation of the members of Christ, that is, of saints who truly believe and obey Christ; though with this congregation many bad and hypocrites are mixed in this life, till the last judgment.' vii.—And the Saxon: "We say then that the visible Church in this life is an assembly of those who embrace the Gospel of Christ and rightly use the Sacraments," &c. xii.]

These illustrations of the phraseology of the Article may be multiplied in any number. And they plainly show that it is not laying down any logical definition what a Church is, but is describing, and, as it were, pointing to the Catholic Church diffused throughout the world; which, being but one, cannot possibly be mistaken, and requires no other account of it beyond this single and majestic one. The ministration of the Word and Sacraments is mentioned as a further note of it. As to the question of its limits, whether Episcopal Succession or whether intercommunion with the whole be necessary to each part of it,—these are questions, most important indeed, but of detail, and are not expressly treated of in the Articles.

This view is further illustrated by the following passage from the Homily for Whitsunday:—

"Our Saviour Christ departing out of the world unto His Father, promised His Disciples to send down another Comforter, that should continue with them for ever, and direct them into all truth. Which thing, to be faithfully and truly performed, the Scriptures do sufficiently bear witness. Neither must we think that this Comforter was either promised, or else given, only to the Apostles, but also *to the universal Church of* Christ, *dispersed through the whole world*. For, unless the Holy Ghost has been always present, governing and preserving the Church from the beginning, it could never have suffered so many and great brunts of affliction and persecution, with so little damage and harm as it hath. And the words of Christ are most plain in this behalf, saying, that 'the Spirit of Truth should abide with them for ever' that 'He would be with them always (He meaneth by grace, virtue, and power) even to the world's end.'

> ❝ *Neither must we think that this Comforter was either promised, or else given, only to the Apostles, but also to the universal Church of Christ, dispersed through the whole world.* ❞

"Also in the prayer that He made to His Father a little before His death, He maketh intercession, not only for Himself and His Apostles, but indifferently for all them that should *believe* in Him through their words, that is, to wit, for His whole Church. Again, St. Paul saith, 'If any man have not the Spirit of Christ, the same is not His.' Also, in the words following: 'We have received the Spirit of adoption, whereby we cry, Abba, Father.' Hereby, then it is evident and plain to all men, that the Holy Ghost was given, not only to the Apostles, but also to the *whole body of* Christ's *congregation*, although not in like form and majesty as He came down at the feast of Pentecost. But now herein standeth the controversy,— whether all men do justly arrogate to themselves the Holy Ghost, or no. The Bishops of Rome have for a long time made a sore challenge thereto, reasoning with themselves after this sort: 'The Holy Ghost,' say they, 'was promised to the Church, and never forsaketh the Church. But we are the chief heads and the principal part of the Church, therefore we have the Holy Ghost for ever: and whatsoever things we decree are undoubted verities and oracles of the Holy Ghost.' That ye may perceive the weakness of this argument, it is needful to teach you, first, what the true Church of Christ is, and then to confer the Church of Rome therewith, to discern how well they agree together. The true Church is *an universal congregation or fellowship of God's faithful and elect people*, built upon the foundation of the Apostles and Prophets, Jesus Christ Himself being the head corner-stone. And it hath always three notes or marks, whereby it is known: pure and sound doctrine, the Sacraments ministered according to Christ's holy institution, and the right use of ecclesiastical discipline. This description of the Church is agreeable both to the Scriptures of God, and also to the doctrine of the ancient Fathers, so that none may justly find fault therewith. Now, if you will compare this with the Church of Rome, not as it was in the beginning, but as it is at present, and hath been for the space of nine hundred years and odd; you shall well perceive the state thereof to be so far wide from the nature of the Church, that nothing can be more."

This passage is in quotes, not for all it contains, but in that respect in which it claims attention, viz. as far as it is an illustration of the Article. It is speaking of the one Catholic Church, not of an abstract idea of a Church which may be multiplied indefinitely in fact; and it uses the same terms of it which the Articles does of "the visible Church." It says that "the true Church is an universal congregation or fellowship of God's faithful and elect people." &c., which as closely corresponds to the *cœtus fidelium*, or "congregation of faithful men" of the Article, as the above descriptions from Fathers or Divines do. Therefore, the *cœtus fidelium* spoken of in the article is not a definition, which **kirk**, or connexion, or other communion maybe made to fall under, but the enunciation of a fact.

kirk Scottish word meaning "church."

For Reflection

1. The excerpt in this chapter quotes several theologians and saints throughout history in describing the Church. Choose three descriptions that are most meaningful to you, and explain why you chose each one.

2. Do you agree that "unless the Holy Ghost has been always present, governing and preserving the Church from the beginning, it could never have suffered so many and great brunts of affliction and persecution, with so little damage and harm as it hath"? Why or why not?

3. Why do you think Newman identified apostolicity and catholicity as the two essential points in his search for the true Church?

16 Fourth Mark: The Church Is Apostolic

Introduction

We have seen in earlier chapters that certain truths exist beyond the realm of human reason or scientific method and technological progress. These truths, such as the Trinity and Incarnation, can only be understood through Divine Revelation. Yet there are other truths that seem to fall somewhere in between what our physical senses tell us about the created world and what God has chosen to reveal to us through Scripture, the teachings of the Apostles, the Tradition of the Church, worship, and the lives of the saints. These truths come from the beauty and intensity of daily living and have the potential to transform our lives if we are able to discern their worth.

What are these truths? That God loves us and has created us for love; that kindness and compassion are the only sensible way of relating to others; that the important things in life cannot be scanned, weighed, or measured; that sin and evil are real and we must help one another endure them patiently and repent of them; that freedom is not a privilege but our right as human beings; and that gratefulness should be our response to God and one another. These truths are reasonable, and yet they do not come from reason. They are divinely inspired yet not explicitly part of an official creed. What are they then? They are human truths, half heavenly, half earthly, and in this chapter's selection, they are expressed through poetry.

In the selections that follow, one of the greatest poets of the twentieth century, T. S. Eliot (1888–1965), speaks to us of fidelity, love, and the Body of Christ through poetic imagery that makes us stop and think. For instance, is the hippopotamus in the first poem a metaphor for the natural world, the animal kingdom, ancient Egypt with its animistic gods and goddesses, or something else? Perhaps it is all of these or something that Eliot never even imagined. Poetic truth, unlike scientific fact, often assumes a meaning of its own beyond what the author intended. This is true not only of poetic truth but also of religious truth and the life of faith, which was one of Eliot's major themes. He was interested in the apostolic traditions of the Church: *The Hippopotamus* begins with an excerpt in Latin (the traditional language of the Church) as a reminder of the Church's stability through the ages. Eliot was also interested in preserving these Church teachings—teachings handed down from the Apostles—while making them accessible to a new generation of Christians: Another short passage, also in Latin, warns of the danger of falling into apathy, as did the Laodiceans.

Even though Eliot does not speak directly about Apostolic Succession or the Marks of the Church, he is clearly concerned about the Church being reborn from its apostolic roots in modern times for the reason that it is one of the few institutions left—perhaps the only one—that can preserve the human element in a world becoming increasingly machinelike. The Church, through its direct connection to its founder, Jesus Christ, has the task of passing on the message of life and salvation. Eliot says in *Choruses from "The Rock"*:

> And all that was good you must fight to keep with
>   hearts as
> devoted as those of your fathers who fought to gain it.
> The Church must be forever building, for it is forever
>   decaying
> within and attacked from without.

In this poem, Eliot is reminding us of the restoration of the Kingdom of Judah (445 BC), but the words are directed to us today so that in our pursuit of the "perfect refrigerator" or any other material possession, we might stop and remember what is truly important.

The Hippopotamus and Excerpts from *Choruses from "The Rock"*

By T. S. Eliot

The Hippopotamus

Similiter et omnes revereantur Diaconos, ut mandatum Jesu Christi; et Epis-
copum, ut Jesum Christum, existentem filium Patris; Presbyteros autem, ut
concilium Dei et conjunctionem Apostolorum. Sine his Ecclesia non vocatur;
de quibus suadeo vos sic habeo.[1]

S. IGNATII AD TRALLIANOS.
And when this epistle is read among you,
cause that it be read also in the church of the Laodiceans.[2]

The broad-backed hippopotamus
Rests on his belly in the mud;
Although he seems so firm to us
He is merely flesh and blood.

Flesh and blood is weak and frail,
Susceptible to nervous shock;
While the True Church can never fail
For it is based upon a rock.

The hippo's feeble steps may err
In compassing material ends,
While the True Church need never stir
To gather in its dividends.
The 'potamus can never reach
The mango on the mango-tree;
But fruits of pomegranate and peach
Refresh the Church from over sea.

At mating time the hippo's voice
Betrays inflexions hoarse and odd,
But every week we hear rejoice
The Church, at being one with God.

The hippopotamus's day
Is passed in sleep; at night he hunts;
God works in a mysterious way—
The Church can sleep and feed at once.

I saw the 'potamus take wing
Ascending from the damp savannas,
And **quiring** angels round him sing
The praise of God, in loud hosannas.

Blood of the Lamb shall wash him clean
And him shall heavenly arms enfold,
Among the saints he shall be seen
Performing on a harp of gold.

He shall be washed as white as snow,
By all the martyr'd virgins kist,
While the True Church remains below
Wrapt in the old **miasmal** mist.

quiring From *quire*, an archaic variation of *choir*.

miasmal Adjective, from the Greek word meaning "to pollute"; related to an atmosphere of corruption.

Excerpt from *Choruses from "The Rock"*

II

Of all that was done in the past, you eat the fruit, either rotten
        or ripe.
And the Church must be forever building, and always decaying,
        and always being restored.
For every ill deed in the past we suffer the consequence:
For sloth, for avarice, gluttony, neglect of the Word of G O D,

For pride, for lechery, treachery, for every act of sin.
And of all that was done that was good, you have the inheritance.
For good and ill deeds belong to a man alone, when he stands
      alone on the other side of death,
But here upon earth you have the reward of the good and ill
      that was done by those who have gone before you.
And all that is ill you may repair if you walk together in humble
      repentance, expiating the sins of your fathers;
And all that was good you must fight to keep with hearts as
      devoted as those of your fathers who fought to gain it.
The Church must be forever building, for it is forever decaying
      within and attacked from without;
For this is the law of life; and you must remember that while
      there is time of prosperity
The people will neglect the Temple, and in time of adversity
      they will decry it.

What life have you if you have not life together?
There is no life that is not in community,
And no community not lived in praise of G O D.
Even the anchorite who meditates alone,
For whom the days and nights repeat the praise of G O D,
Prays for the Church, the Body of Christ incarnate.
And now you live dispersed on ribbon roads,
And no man knows or cares who is his neighbour
Unless his neighbour makes too much disturbance,
But all dash to and fro in motor cars,
Familiar with the roads and settled nowhere.
Nor does the family even move about together,

> 66 *And the Church must be forever*
> *building, and always decaying,*
> *and always being restored.* 99

But every son would have his motor
    cycle,
And daughters ride away on casual
    pillions.

Much to cast down, much to build,
    much to restore;
Let the work not delay, time and the
    arm not waste;
Let the clay be dug from the pit, let
    the saw cut the stone,
Let the fire not be quenched in the
    forge.

III

The Word of the LORD came unto
    me, saying:
O miserable cities of designing men,
O wretched generation of enlightened men,
Betrayed in the mazes of your ingenuities,
Sold by the proceeds of your proper inventions:
I have given you hands which you turn from worship,
I have given you speech, for endless **palaver**,
I have given you my Law, and you set up commissions,
I have given you lips, to express friendly
    sentiments,
I have given you hearts, for reciprocal
    distrust.
I have given you power of choice, and
    you only alternate
Between futile speculation and
    unconsidered action.
Many are engaged in writing books
    and printing them,

Anchorite

The word *anchorite* derives from *anchor*, that is, fixed or held to one place. This form of monastic life was popular during the Early and High Middle Ages (from approximately AD 400 to 1300). An anchorite is a person committed to living a life of prayer and fasting apart from others, in a small room or cell, either in a remote area or attached to a church. The cell of an anchorite is called an *anchorage*.

pillion Chiefly British, originally meaning a saddle for a woman; in modern times a motorcycle or bicycle saddle for a passenger.

palaver From the Latin *parabola*, meaning speech; a discussion, sometimes with the connotation of verbose or idle talk, misleading speech.

Many desire to see their names in print,
Many read nothing but the race reports.
Much is your reading, but not the Word of G O D,
Much is your building, but not the House of G O D.
Will you build me a house of plaster, with corrugated roofing,
To be filled with a litter of Sunday newspapers?

O weariness of men who turn from G O D
To the grandeur of your mind and the glory of your action,
To arts and inventions and daring enterprises,
To schemes of human greatness thoroughly discredited,
Binding the earth and the water to your service,
Exploiting the seas and developing the mountains,
Dividing the stars into common and preferred,
Engaged in devising the perfect refrigerator,
Engaged in working out a rational morality,
Engaged in printing as many books as possible,
Plotting of happiness and flinging empty bottles,
Turning from your vacancy to fevered enthusiasm
For nation or race or what you call humanity;
Though you forget the way to the Temple,
There is one who remembers the way to your door:
Life you may evade, but Death you shall not.
You shall not deny the Stranger.

VI

It is hard for those who have never known persecution,
And who have never known a Christian,
To believe these tales of Christian persecution.
It is hard for those who live near a Bank
To doubt the security of their money.
It is hard for those who live near a Police Station
To believe in the triumph of violence.
Do you think that the Faith has conquered the World
And that lions no longer need keepers?

Do you need to be told that whatever has been, can still be?

Do you need to be told that even such modest attainments

As you can boast in the way of polite society

Will hardly survive the Faith to which they owe their significance?

Men! polish your teeth on rising and retiring;

Women! polish your fingernails:

You polish the tooth of the dog and the talon of the cat.

Why should men love the Church? Why should they love
    her laws?

She tells them of Life and Death, and of all that they would forget.

She is tender where they would be hard, and hard where
    they like to be soft.

She tells them of Evil and Sin, and other unpleasant facts.

They constantly try to escape

From the darkness outside and within

By dreaming of systems so perfect that no one will need to be
    good.

But the man that is will shadow

The man that pretends to be.

And the Son of Man was not crucified once for all,

The blood of the martyrs not shed once for all,

The lives of the Saints not given once for all:

But the Son of Man is crucified always

And there shall be Martyrs and Saints.

And if blood of Martyrs is to flow on the steps

We must first build the steps;

And if the Temple is to be cast down

We must first build the Temple.

Endnotes

1. Latin: "Equally, it is for the rest of you to hold the deacons in as great respect as Jesus Christ; just as you should also look on the bishop as a type of the Father, and the clergy as the Apostolic circle forming His council; for without these three orders no church has any right to the name. I am sure these are your own feelings too." From the Letter to the Trallians, written by Saint Ignatius of Antioch (first century CE [AD]), an early Christian theologian.
2. From Colossians 4:16. See also the Book of Revelation 3:15–18, where the Laodiceans are described as "neither hot nor cold" but rather lukewarm Christians.

For Reflection

1. Eliot has a biting critique of modern society that, he says, has turned away from God and become obsessed with its own "arts and inventions and daring enterprises." Do you agree? Why or why not?

2. How does Eliot understand community and its relationship to the Church?

3. Eliot asks, "Why should men love the Church?" How would you answer his question?

4. What is your favorite line or set of lines from the Eliot selections in this chapter? Explain your choice.

Part 4
The Church in the World

17 Fleeing Toward the Future

Introduction

In this excerpt about the Church of the future, Belgian theologian Edward Schillebeeckx (1914–2009) calls us to be a people of faith actively engaged *in* the world and concerned about the social, economic, and political ills that plague us, but not *of* the world. By this he means that in the past, we tended to emphasize the cultic aspects of our faith—liturgy, doctrine, Sacraments, and internal governance—but neglected the social dimension of the Church and its role in the historical development of peoples and their progress toward greater freedom. The Church of the future must have a broader sense of its mission and take an active part in history, becoming Christ's presence to the rest of humanity. After all, the purpose of the Church, her "grace and vocation" is to preach the Good News of Christ to everyone (Pope Paul VI, *Evangelii Nuntiandi*, 14). This includes the transformation of human systems that work against Christ's message of salvation, grace, and freedom.

Related to this is what Schillebeeckx has identified as the "radical self-emptying" that

> ### *Evangelii Nuntiandi (Evangelization in the Modern World)*
>
> Pope Paul VI wrote this Apostolic Exhortation in 1975 to celebrate the tenth anniversary of the closing of Vatican Council II. It reiterates the need for an evangelization that not only preaches the Gospel to the whole world but also lives it. This includes challenging injustice and fostering the freedom of all people. Yet, life in Christian community—community as lived witness to others—is at the core of Gospel living, for "the Christian community is never closed in upon itself" (15).

the Church needs to do so the message of salvation can "break through" to the entire world. What is this self-emptying and why does he call it that? *Self-emptying* refers to love. There are all kinds of love, of course: the love of parents for their children, siblings for one another, friends for one another, and the intimate love of marriage. There is also the love of Christ for his Church. No matter what kind of love, however—but especially the love of Christ for the Church and the Church for the world—it must be a love that does not hold back. It must be a fully committed love that does not keep something in reserve "just in case" something goes wrong. It is a love that gives everything and risks all for the beloved. Schillebeeckx calls the Church to this self-emptying kind of love (in Greek, **kenosis**), because it is precisely the kind of love that Christ has for the Church and is immortalized in the famous liturgical hymn from Philippians 2:5–11.

It is worth noting that Schillebeeckx wrote this excerpt in 1967, at the height of the Civil Rights movement in the United States. Interestingly, the themes of freedom, equality, human rights, and the dignity of people are issues that we are still concerned about today and appear in the news daily. As you read this excerpt from one of the Church's most prolific and inspirational theologians of the twentieth century, see if you can identify commonalities with the world and Church of today, as well as your own life. Ask yourself if Schillebeeckx's vision for the Church of the future has become a reality.

> **kenosis** From the Greek, meaning "self-emptying" or "giving up of oneself." Theologically and liturgically, it refers to the Word of God's self-emptying in becoming man. Schillebeeckx offers it as a model for the work of the Church in the world.

Excerpt from "The Church in the World Community"

By Edward Schillebeeckx

Nowadays, Christianity is discovering the "political" dimension of Christian charity and the worldly dimensions of Christianity. The inspiration here comes from the present situation in the world and from contact with the Bible and especially with the Old Testament. In the past, Christians tended to live in a separate little world of the spirit, where God and the "soul" of man made asides to each other. The Bible, however, teaches us that God is active in the whole world of men and that the church is called to share in this activity of God in the world itself. In this age, God seems to be accomplishing more through men like Martin Luther King, for example, than through the church. As Harvey Cox so rightly said, "We Christians have been a very talkative people, talkative to the point of verbosity." We Christians used to interpret the world differently from non-Christians, but we did not transform it—and this is what really matters. The church must show what the future world will be. And here we are confronted with the mystery of Christianity, which **relativizes** and at the same time **radicalizes** man's work for a better world here on earth. The church therefore has to stimulate us continuously to transcend ourselves. In her liturgy, she has to celebrate the unnamed future, while, in the world, she has to prepare for this future. Non-Christians often leap into the breach to bring the biblical *šālôm* into the world, while Christians are conspicuous by their absence. On the other hand, those Christians who are actively beginning to make this secular dimension of Christianity really true are quickly characterized as "social gospel" Christians. Of course, their emphasis is often one-sided because of their reaction to the "unworldly" church, just as, in the past, a one-sided stress was placed on the cultic aspects of the church.

> 66 *The church therefore has to stimulate us continuously to transcend ourselves. In her liturgy, she has to celebrate the unnamed future, while, in the world, she has to prepare for this future.* 99

It is above all the task of theologians to draw attention to every one-sided emphasis, whether his words are welcome or not. He has, for example, to warn Christians if the radicalization of their commitment to this world is correctly taken into account, but the relativization of this commitment is suppressed, so that the absolute character of man's history here on earth is disregarded and man himself is ultimately misrepresented. On the other hand, however, every period in human history calls for its special emphases. And then we may ask ourselves whether Christians ought not to be on the side of the great social, economic and political revolutions which are taking place in the modern world, not simply going along, as critics, with the revolutions, but as people taking (a critical) part in them. In this case, the real demand made by the present situation in the world may be for Christians to stress, perhaps one-sidedly, this worldly dimension of Christianity. The dangers inherent in such a necessary, but one-sided emphasis must therefore be obviated by an equally one-sided emphasis on contemplative monastic life (in a new form), which is also equally necessary to the totality of Christianity.

Both its relativization and its radicalization of all commitment to man in this world characterize Christianity as a radical self-emptying. In this sense, Christianity is a radically committed love which cannot justify itself, which has again and again to transcend its achievement in this world and which has again and again to give itself away in profound darkness in a self-emptying which often seems to be in vain in this world, but which is nonetheless so radical that it is precisely in this giving away of itself for the benefit of others that the very essence of the kingdom of God breaks through into our world. But this is already the kingdom of God itself—only the form of this present world passes, nothing of what has been achieved in the world by man's radical love for his fellow men. All this implies faith in the absolute God, whose being is the negation

relativizes Treats as relative, not as an absolute.

radicalizes Related to *radical*; literally, "from the roots"; makes essential.

šālôm (shalom) From the Hebrew, meaning "peace," "well-being," and "completeness." In the Old Testament, God's peace brings fulfillment and harmony. Related to the Arabic *salaam*.

of everything that seems to be in vain. Everything that seems, from the human point of view, to be in vain is made meaningful and not ultimately in vain by faith in the absolute God and, in this faith, man is not an anonymous element in history and does not, as is affirmed by an authentically atheistic commitment to a better world, pass forever into oblivion. But, for man, this Christian attitude is a mystery that cannot be rationalized. It is an active surrender to the mystery of God and therefore to the mystery of man. It is a mystery which, as God's "Amen" or "Yes" (2 Cor 1:20) to man, appeared in a veiled form in the man Jesus, the Christ. The Christian does not flee from the world, but flees with the world towards the future. He takes the world with him towards the absolute future which is God himself for man.

For Reflection

1. How can the Church "share in the activity of God in the world"?

2. Schillebeeckx says that "we Christians used to interpret the world differently from non-Christians, but we did not transform it—and this is what really matters. The church must show what the future world will be." What did he mean by this? Do you agree with him? Why or why not?

3. What does Schillebeeckx see as the mystery of Christianity? How does it both relativize and radicalize our work on earth?

4. What does it mean to suggest, as Schillebeeckx does, that because of our faith in God, nothing is in vain?

18 "Homesick at Home"

Introduction

G. K. Chesterton (1874–1936), an English writer and theologian who, like John Henry Newman, left the Anglican Church to become a Roman Catholic, offers a view of the Christian faith at odds with a Christianity that seeks to be open to the world and popular culture in order to influence it from within. In this excerpt from his popular book *Orthodoxy*, he refers to the world and the Church, or Christianity, as two "unmanageable machines" that at first glance do not seem to go together. The world has its own rationality, one of cause and effect, whose laws are fixed by the rhythms of the natural universe and elemental forces such as gravity, light, and magnetism. The Church, on the other hand, asks us to believe things that do not make sense in the conventional understanding of the word. What things? These things: that one achieves life through death, riches through poverty, joy through suffering, and self-fulfillment through loving service to others, and that Christ is the Son of God, fully divine yet fully human.

Chesterton is objecting to the attempt, common during his time, in which scientific reasoning and method were dominant, to merge the two worlds or to define Christianity against the backdrop of science. He believed that doing so might make religion palatable to modern sensibilities but would dilute the richness and sheer power of the world of faith. Rather than argue for Christianity's compatibility with science or the world, he goes in the other direction and emphasizes its differences. This gives him not only relief but optimism. The optimism of the Christian, unlike optimism in general, is that one need not hide his or her differences from the rest of the world and can feel at home even though not at home.

This is similar to what has been presented in this book so far about Christians being *in* the world but not *of* the world.

In his inimitable fashion, Chesterton takes this a step further by saying that human beings are "a monstrosity" and that he was right "in feeling all things as odd, for I myself was at once worse and better than all things." This is a judgment of himself as a person, as well as an assessment of humanity and a recognition that we are saved and sinful at the same time, to paraphrase Martin Luther. Chesterton attributes this to the Fall from Grace that occurred with Adam and Eve and has been humanity's inheritance ever since. This Fall from Grace accounts for much of what we find as paradoxical; for instance, that God is personal, yet we are separated from him, and that "somehow one must love the world without being worldly." Chesterton would probably agree with this saying in regard to the Church's mission: Christians are called to comfort the afflicted and afflict the comfortable. In this excerpt Chesterton warns us that we should not expect to get too comfortable, to be too much at home, in this world. In a sense Chesterton's observation is a relief for all Christians trying to live lives of authenticity and holiness, because it is a call to be real, acknowledge our flaws, and make the best of this world as shipwrecked voyagers far from home.

Excerpt from *Orthodoxy*
By G. K. Chesterton

The Flag of the World

According to most philosophers, God in making the world enslaved it. According to Christianity, in making it, He set it free. God had written, not so much a poem, but rather a play; a play he had planned as perfect, but which had necessarily been left to human actors and stage-managers, who had since made a great mess of it. I will discuss the truth of this theorem later. Here I have only to point out with what a startling smoothness it passed the dilemma we have discussed in this chapter. In this way at least one could be both happy and indignant without degrading one's self to be either a pessimist or an optimist. On this system one could fight all the forces of existence without deserting the flag of existence. One could be at peace with the universe and yet be at war with the world. St. George could still fight the dragon, however big the monster bulked in the cosmos, though he were bigger than the mighty cities or bigger than the everlasting hills. If he were as big as the world he could yet be killed in the name of the world. St. George had not to consider any obvious odds or proportions in the scale of things, but only the original secret of their design. He can shake his sword at the dragon, even if it is everything; even if the empty heavens over his head are only the huge arch of its open jaws.

> **Saint George and the Dragon**
>
> A mythic tale thought to have originated during the Crusades about a knight who saves a maiden from a dragon. The maiden is sometimes portrayed as having been offered as a sacrifice to the dragon, which lives at the bottom of a lake. The battle between Saint George and the dragon has been depicted in numerous paintings, sculptures, and stained-glass artworks. It has also been interpreted as a metaphor for the defeat of Satan and the inner transformation of the soul.

And then followed an experience impossible to describe. It was as if I had been blundering about since my birth with two huge and unmanageable machines, of different shapes and without apparent connection—the world and the Christian tradition. I had found this hole in the world: the fact that one must somehow find a way of loving the world without trusting it; somehow one must love the world without being worldly. I found this projecting feature of Christian theology, like a sort of hard spike, the dogmatic insistence that God was personal, and had made a world separate from Himself. The spike of dogma fitted exactly into the hole in the world—it had evidently been meant to go there—and then the strange thing began to happen. When once these two parts of the two machines had come together, one after another, all the other parts fitted and fell in with an eerie exactitude. I could hear bolt after bolt over all the machinery falling into its place with a kind of click of relief. Having got one part right, all the other parts were repeating that rectitude, as clock after clock strikes noon. Instinct after instinct was answered by doctrine after doctrine. Or, to vary the metaphor, I was like one who had advanced into a hostile country to take one high fortress. And when that fort had fallen the whole country surrendered and turned solid behind me. The whole land was lit up, as it were, back to the first fields of my childhood. All those blind fancies of boyhood which . . . I have tried in vain to trace on the darkness, became suddenly transparent and sane. I was right when I felt that roses were red by some sort of choice: it was the divine choice. I was right when I felt that I would almost rather say that grass was the wrong colour than say it must by necessity have been that colour: it might verily have been any other. My sense that happiness hung on the crazy thread of a condition did mean something when all was said: it meant the whole doctrine of the Fall. Even those dim and shapeless monsters of notions which I have not been able to describe, much less defend, stepped quietly into their places like colossal **caryatides** of the creed. The fancy that the cosmos was not vast and void, but small and cosy, had a fulfilled significance now, for anything that is a work of art must be small in the sight of the artist; to God the stars might be only small and dear, like diamonds. And my haunting instinct that somehow good was not merely a tool to be used, but a relic to be guarded, like the goods from **Crusoe's ship**—even that had been the wild whisper of something originally wise, for, according to Christianity, we were indeed the survivors of a wreck, the crew of a golden ship that had gone down before the beginning of the world.

But the important matter was this, that it entirely reversed the reason for optimism. And the instant the reversal was made it felt like the abrupt case when a bone is put back in the socket. I had often called myself an optimist, to avoid the too evident blasphemy of pessimism. But all the optimism of the age had been false and disheartening for this reason, that it had always been trying to prove that we fit in to the world.

caryatides From the Greek, meaning "priestess"; draped female figures used as columns to support a roof or a section of a building.

Crusoe's ship Refers to a 1799 novel by Daniel Defoe, *Robinson Crusoe*. The main character, Crusoe, is shipwrecked on an island in the Caribbean Sea. The novel tells the story of his survival.

The Christian optimism is based on the fact that we do *not* fit in to the world. I had tried to be happy by telling myself that man is an animal, like any other which sought its meat from God. But now I really was happy, for I had learnt that man is a monstrosity. I had been right in feeling all things as odd, for I myself was at once worse and better than all things. The optimist's pleasure was prosaic, for it dwelt on the naturalness of every-

> *According to Christianity, we were indeed the survivors of a wreck, the crew of a golden ship that had gone down before the beginning of the world.*

thing; the Christian pleasure was poetic, for it dwelt on the unnaturalness of everything in the light of the supernatural. The modern philosopher had told me again and again that I was in the right place, and I had still felt depressed even in acquiescence. But I had heard that I was in the *wrong* place, and my soul sang for joy, like a bird in spring. The knowledge found out and illuminated forgotten chambers in the dark house of infancy. I knew now why grass had always seemed to me as queer as the green beard of a giant, and why I could feel homesick at home.

For Reflection

1. How does the doctrine of the Fall figure into Chesterton's understanding of living in the world?

2. Do you agree with Chesterton that Christians do not "fit in to the world"? Explain your answer.

3. Why could Chesterton "feel homesick at home"? In what ways are you, as both a human being and a Christian, "homesick at home"? Explain your answer.

19 "The Sublime Dignity of the Human Person"

Introduction

Gaudium et Spes (1965) is the Latin title of a document from the Second Vatican Council (see chapter 9, "A Church in Exile") that addresses the role of the Church in the modern world. The Latin title comes from the first two words of the document, which translate as "joy and hope." In effect, *Gaudium et Spes* proclaims that the joy and hope, as well as the "grief and anguish," of people everywhere are the direct concern of the Church today, which cannot be set apart or isolated from the world but must be involved intimately in those things that are important to people and have the greatest effect on their lives. These include aspects of life that before the Council were not usually thought of as having to do with faith, such as work, money, technology, social relations, human freedom, and sexuality. However, in *Gaudium et Spes* the Church recognizes that whatever affects people in their daily struggle to be loving and fully human is not alien to faith but is at the heart of Christian discipleship.

Not everyone agrees. Some people think that religion is a private affair and should be kept out of daily life. Others think that religion has proven to be harmful and the root of violence and hatred. They point to the rise of fundamentalism in all its forms and in various regions of the world, such as the Middle East. Still others say that they respect religion but that it should be barred from public discourse and politics. This is why *Gaudium et Spes* argues eloquently for the engagement of the Church in the social, political, and cultural affairs of humanity, insisting on basic principles and freedoms for all people. Among these is the freedom to believe in God, to worship with like-minded men and women, and to safeguard human dignity and freedom, which the Church sees as under attack from atheism and the belief that human beings are accidents and human history the result of random events. The document speaks of the Gospel as the best way to ensure human freedom and worth, referring to "the sublime dignity of human persons, who stand above all things and whose rights and duties are universal" (26). In this way, *Gaudium et Spes* sees human beings not as accidental byproducts but the deliberate fruit of God's love.

Like the *Dogmatic Constitution on the Church (Lumen Gentium)*, *Gaudium et Spes* is a

> **Constitution**
>
> In the Church, a constitution is a document produced by a Church Council that carries binding authority and represents the consensus of the Pope, the bishops, and the entire People of God. The *Dogmatic Constitution on the Church (Lumen Gentium)* is a *dogmatic* constitution, addressing points of dogma or formal teaching. The *Dogmatic Constitution on the Church in the Modern World (Gaudium et Spes)* is a *pastoral* constitution concerned with how certain dogmatic truths are lived by Christians and shared with the rest of the world.

constitution, which means that it carries tremendous weight in the teachings of the Church. As you read this excerpt, see if you can find common themes with readings from earlier chapters, particularly regarding freedom and the Church's attempt to realize the kingdom of God on earth through a social order "founded in truth, built on justice, and enlivened by love" (26). You might also ask yourself whether the rights it lists, such as the right to education, to have a family, or to work in a decent and meaningful way, have changed since 1965.

Excerpt from *Pastoral Constitution on the Church in the Modern World (Gaudium et Spes)*

By the Second Vatican Council

Chapter II: The Human Community

Communitarian Nature of the Human Vocation: God's Design

24. God, who has a parent's care for all of us, desired that all men and women should form one family and deal with each other as brothers and sisters. All, in fact, are destined to the very same end, namely God himself, since they have been created in the likeness of God, who "made from one every nation of humankind who live on all the face of the earth" (Acts 17:26). Love of God and of one's neighbor, then, is the first and greatest commandment. Scripture teaches us that love of God cannot be separated from love of one's neighbor: "Any other commandment [is] summed up in this sentence: 'You shall love your neighbor as yourself . . .' therefore love is the fulfilling of the law" (Rom 13:9–10; see 1 Jn 4:20). It goes without saying that this is a matter of the utmost importance to people who are coming to rely more and more on each other and to a world which is becoming more unified every day.

Furthermore, the Lord Jesus, when praying to the Father "that they may all be one . . . even as we are one" (Jn 17:21–22), has opened up new horizons closed to human reason by indicating that there is a certain similarity between the union existing among the divine persons and the union of God's children in truth and love. It follows, then, that if human beings are the only creatures on earth that God has wanted for their own sake, they can fully discover their true selves only in sincere self-giving. (See Lk 17:33.)

Person and Society: Interdependence

25. The fact that human beings are social by nature indicates that the betterment of the person and the improvement of society depend on each

other. Insofar as humanity by its very nature stands completely in need of life in society,[1] it is and it ought to be the beginning, the subject and the object of every social organization. Life in society is not something accessory to humanity: through their dealings with others, through mutual service, and through fraternal and sororal dialogue, men and women develop all their talents and become able to rise to their destiny.

Among the social ties necessary for humanity's development, some correspond more immediately to our innermost nature—the family, for instance, and the political community; others are freely chosen. Nowadays, for various reasons, mutual relationships and interdependence increase from day to day and give rise to a variety of associations and organizations, both public and private. Socialization, as it is called, is not without its dangers, but it brings with it many advantages for the strengthening and betterment of human qualities and for the protection of human rights.[2]

On the one hand, in fulfilling their calling, including their religious calling, men and women are greatly helped by life in society, on the other hand, however, it cannot be denied that they are often turned away from the good and towards evil by the social environment in which they live and in which they have been immersed since their birth. Without doubt frequent upheavals in the social order are in part the result of economic, political, and social tensions. But at a deeper level they come from selfishness and pride, two things which contaminate the atmosphere of society as well. As it is, human beings are prone to evil, but whenever they are confronted with an environment where the effects of sin are to be found, they are exposed to further inducements to sin, which can be overcome only by unremitting effort with the help of grace.

The Common Good

26. Because of the increasingly close interdependence which is gradually extending to the entire world, we are today witnessing an extension of the role of the common good, which is the sum total of social conditions which allow people, either as groups or as individuals, to reach their fulfillment more fully and more easily. The resulting rights and obligations are consequently the concern of the entire human race. Every group must take

into account the needs and legitimate aspirations of every other group, and even those of the human family as a whole.[3]

At the same time, however, there is a growing awareness of the sublime dignity of human persons, who stand above all things and whose rights and duties are universal and inviolable. They ought, therefore, to have ready access to all that is necessary for living a genuinely human life: for example, food, clothing, housing, the right freely to choose their state of life and set up a family, the right to education, work, to their good name, to respect, to proper knowledge, the right to act according to the dictates of conscience and to safeguard their privacy, and rightful freedom, including freedom of religion.

The social order and its development must constantly yield to the good of the person, since the order of things must be subordinate to the order of persons and not the other way around, as the Lord suggested when he said that the Sabbath was made for men and women and not men and women for the Sabbath. (Mk 2:27) The social order requires constant improvement: it must be founded in truth, built on justice, and enlivened by love: it should grow in freedom toward a more humane equilibrium.[4] If these objectives are to be attained there will first have to be a renewal of attitudes and far-reaching social changes.

The Spirit of God, who, with wonderful providence, directs the course of time and renews the face of the earth, assists at this development. The ferment of the Gospel has aroused and continues to arouse in human hearts an unquenchable thirst for human dignity.

Respect for the Human Person

27. Coming to topics which are practical and of some urgency, the council lays stress on respect for the human person: everybody should look upon his or her neighbor (without any exception) as another self, bearing in mind especially their neighbor's life and the means needed for a dignified way of life, (see Jas 2:15–16) lest they follow the example of the rich man who ignored Lazarus, who was poor. (See Lk 16:19–31.)

Today, there is an inescapable duty to make ourselves the neighbor of every individual, without exception, and to take positive steps to help a neighbor whom we encounter, whether that neighbor be an elderly person abandoned by everyone, a foreign worker who suffers the injustice of being despised, a refugee, an illegitimate child wrongly suffering for sin of which the child is innocent, or a starving human being who awakens our conscience by calling to mind the words

> " *Everybody should look upon his or her neighbor (without any exception) as another self, bearing in mind especially their neighbor's life and the means needed for a dignified way of life.* "

of Christ: "As you did it to one of the least of these my brothers or sisters, you did it to me" (Mt 25:40).

The varieties of crime are numerous: all offenses against life itself, such as murder, genocide, abortion, euthanasia and willful suicide; all violations of the integrity of the human person, such as mutilation, physical and mental torture, undue psychological pressures; all offenses against human dignity, such as subhuman living conditions, arbitrary imprisonment, deportation, slavery, prostitution, the selling of women and children, degrading working conditions where people are treated as mere tools for profit rather than free and responsible persons: all these and the like are criminal: they poison civilization; and they debase the perpetrators more than the victims and militate against the honor of the creator.

Respect and Love for Enemies

28. Those also have a claim on our respect and charity who think and act differently from us in social, political, and religious matters. In fact, the more deeply, through courtesy and love, we come to understand their ways of thinking, the more easily will we be able to enter into dialogue with them.

Love and courtesy of this kind should not, of course, make us indifferent to truth and goodness. Love, in fact, impels the followers of Christ to proclaim to everyone the truth which saves. But we must distinguish between the error (which must always be rejected) and the people in error, who never lose their dignity as persons even though they flounder amid false or inadequate religious ideas.[5] God, who alone is the judge and the searcher of hearts, forbids us to pass judgment on the inner guilt of others. (See Lk 6:37–38; Mt 7:1–2; Rom 2:1–11, 14:10–12.)

The teaching of Christ even demands that we forgive injury, (see Mt 5:43–47) and the precept of love, which is the commandment of the New Law, includes all our enemies: "You have heard that it was said, 'You shall love your neighbor and hate your enemy.' But I say to you, love your enemies, do good to them that hate you; and pray for those who persecute and calumniate you" (Mt 5:43–44).

Endnotes

1. See St. Thomas Aquinas, I Ethic., Lect. 1.
2. See John XXIII, Encyclical. *Mater et Magistra* 15 May 1961: *AAS* 53 (1961), p. 418. See also Pius XI, Encyclical *Quadragesimo Anno,* 15 May 1931: *AAS* 23 (1931), p. 222 ff.
3. See John XXIII, Encyclical *Mater et Magistra: AAS* 53 (1961), p.417.
4. Cf. John XXIII, Encyclical *Pacem in Terris: AAS* 55 (1963), p. 266.
5. Cf. John XXIII, Encyclical *Pacem in Terris: AAS* 55 (1963), pp. 299 and 300.

For Reflection

1. Why should the Church be involved in the "secular" sphere as outlined by *Gaudium et Spes*?

2. *Gaudium et Spes* states that the root causes of social ills are selfishnessand pride, "two things which contaminate the atmosphere of society" (25). How do you see selfishness and pride at work in the world?

3. What does it mean to say that human beings "stand above all things" (26)? What rights and duties come with that status?

4. What is the relationship between love and truth as presented in the document?

20 Science and Faith: Is There a Problem?

Introduction

"Incongruous places often inspire anomalous stories. In early 1984, I spent several nights at the Vatican housed in a hotel built for itinerant priests." Thus begins Stephen Jay Gould, a paleontologist and self-described "Jewish agnostic," in a story recounting the time he attended a conference sponsored by the Pontifical Academy of Sciences in Rome. The conference was studying the effects of a possible nuclear winter, but what fascinated Gould was the interest, on the part of many he had met, in evolution versus the concept of creationism, which was in the headlines at the time. Many at the Vatican conference believed, like Gould, that no conflict exists between faith and science (including the theory of evolution) and the scriptural accounts of Creation in Genesis. They simply represent two very distinct ways of understanding human existence and the origin of life. In fact, Pope Saint John Paul II has stated: "There exists two realms of knowledge, one that has its source in revelation and one that reason can discover by its own power. To the latter belong especially the experimental sciences and philosophy.

The distinction between the two realms of knowledge ought not to be understood as opposition. The two realms are not altogether foreign to each other; they have points of contact. The methodologies proper to each make it possible to bring out different aspects of reality" ("Lessons of the Galileo Case").

> **Creationism**
>
> Creationism is the belief that the two Creation accounts in the Book of Genesis (1:1–23; 2:4–25) are literally and factually true, thus conflicting with the theory of evolution. This belief is popular among certain fundamentalist Christians.

Magisterium(a)

From the Latin *magister*, meaning "teacher," *Magisterium* refers to the authoritative teaching office of the Church, consisting of all bishops, in communion with the Pope. The Magisterium interprets Divine Revelation, which consists of Sacred Scripture and Sacred Tradition. Gould uses *magisterium* as a term for "teaching authority" in general, including that of the Church and of science.

Gould explains these two methodologies as the result of what he calls the "standard model of non-overlapping magisteria (NOMA)." According to Gould, this means that the Church's expertise lies within the boundaries of morality, ethics, and spirituality (one magisterium or teaching authority), while science is concerned with the raw data of physical existence and possible reasons for how existence got that way (another magisterium). These two magisteria sit next to each other, come close to each other, nearly touch as if **asymptotes**, but never cross the boundary separating them. To be sure, Gould's understanding of the Church's expertise is a judgment made from someone not within the faith (otherwise, he would know that ethics and morality are part of the life of faith but not its entirety). And there are areas in which religion and science may have already crossed the boundary, as in studies of life after death, dark energy, and the origin of the universe. Still, the idea that faith and science are not in conflict and have never been is an effective way to liberate both to pursue their respective interests. Science is not hampered by dogmatic considerations, and faith can explore its own proper dimensions without having to prove that its texts and worship are "scientific," that is to say, that there is a truth beyond the kind of facts that can be verified by science.

asymptote From a Greek word meaning "not meeting." Used in analytical geometry, it describes the close relationship between a line and a curve. As each extends into infinity while next to the other, the distance between them gets closer and closer, but they never touch.

In the following excerpt, note the similarities

between Gould's position (which he identifies as NOMA) and the quotation from Pope John Paul II, on page 133.

Excerpt from "Non-overlapping Magisteria," from *Leonardo's Mountain of Clams and the Diet of Worms*

By Stephen Jay Gould

I am not, personally, a believer or a religious man in any sense of institutional commitment or practice. But I have great respect for religion, and the subject has always fascinated me, beyond almost all others (with a few exceptions, like evolution and paleontology). Much of this fascination lies in the stunning historical paradox that organized religion has fostered, throughout Western history, both the most unspeakable horrors and the most heartrending examples of human goodness in the face of personal danger. (The evil, I believe, lies in an occasional confluence of religion with secular power. The Catholic Church has sponsored its share of horrors, from Inquisitions to liquidations—but only because this institution held great secular power during so much of Western history. When my folks held such sway, more briefly and in Old Testament times, we committed similar atrocities with the same rationales.)

I believe, with all my heart, in a respectful, even loving, concordat between our magisteria—the NOMA concept. NOMA represents a principled position on moral and intellectual grounds, not a merely diplomatic solution. NOMA also cuts both ways. If religion can no longer dictate the nature of factual conclusions residing properly within the magisterium of science, then scientists cannot claim higher insight into moral truth from any superior knowledge of the world's empirical constitution. This mutual humility leads to important practical consequences in a world of such diverse passions.

Religion is too important for too many people to permit any dismissal or denigration of the comfort still sought by many folks from theology. I may, for example, privately suspect that papal insistence on the divine infusion of the soul represents a sop to our fears, a device for maintaining

interloper An intruder.

a belief in human superiority within an evolutionary world offering no privileged position to any creature. But I also know that the subject of souls lies outside the magisterium of science. My world cannot prove or disprove such a notion, and the concept of souls cannot threaten or impact my domain. Moreover, while I cannot personally accept the Catholic view of souls, I surely honor the metaphorical value of such a concept both for grounding moral discussion, and for expressing what we most value about human potentiality: our decency, our care, and all the ethical and intellectual struggles that the evolution of consciousness imposed upon us.

As a moral position (and therefore not as a deduction from my knowledge of nature's factuality), I prefer the "cold bath" theory that nature can be truly "cruel" and "indifferent"—in the utterly inappropriate terms of our ethical discourse—because nature does not exist for us, didn't know we were coming (we are, after all, **interlopers** of the latest geological moment), and doesn't give a damn about us (speaking metaphorically). I regard such a position as liberating, not depressing, because we then gain the capacity to conduct moral discourse—and nothing could be more important—in our own terms, free from the delusion that we might read moral truth passively from nature's factuality.

But I recognize that such a position frightens many people, and that a more spiritual view of nature retains broad appeal (acknowledging the factuality of evolution, but still seeking some intrinsic meaning in human terms, and from the magisterium of religion). I do appreciate, for example, the struggles of a man who wrote to *The New York Times* on November 3, 1996, to declare both his pain and his endorsement of John Paul's statement:[1]

> Pope John Paul II's acceptance of evolution touches the doubt in my heart. The problem of pain and suffering in a world created by a God who is all love and light is hard enough to bear, even if one is a creationist. But at least a creationist can say that the original creation, coming from the hand of God, was good, harmonious, innocent and gentle. What can one say about evolution, even a spiritual theory of evolution? Pain

and suffering, mindless cruelty and terror are its means of creation. Evolution's engine is the grinding of predatory teeth upon the screaming, living flesh and bones of prey. . . . If evolution be true, my faith has rougher seas to sail.

I don't agree with this man, but we could have a terrific argument. I would push the "cold bath" theory; he would (presumably) advocate the theme of inherent spiritual meaning in nature, however opaque the signal. But we would both be enlightened and filled with better understanding of these deep and ultimately unanswerable issues. Here, I believe, lies the greatest strength and necessity of NOMA, the non-overlapping magisteria of science and religion. NOMA permits—indeed enjoins—the prospect of respectful discourse, of constant input from both magisteria toward the common goal of wisdom. If human beings can lay claim to anything special, we evolved as the only creatures that must ponder and talk. Pope John Paul II would surely point out to me that his magisterium has always recognized this uniqueness, for John's gospel begins by stating *in principio erat verbum*—in the beginning was the word.

> *Here, I believe, lies the greatest strength and necessity of NOMA, the non-overlapping magisteria of science and religion. NOMA permits—indeed enjoins—the prospect of respectful discourse, of constant input from both magisteria toward the common goal of wisdom.*

Endnote

1. Editor's note: This refers to the *Address of Pope John Paul II to the Pontifical Academy of Sciences*, October 22, 1996, on the topic of evolution, in which he noted the acceptance of scientific evidence for the theory (or theories) of evolution and also affirmed the biblical revelation that we are created in the image and likeness of God. (See Genesis 1:27–29.) An English translation of this speech can be found in *Origins*, Vol. 26, No. 22, November 14, 1996.

For Reflection

1. What is the Catholic Church's position on evolution, as stated by Pope Saint John Paul II and referenced by the Gould article (see endnote 1)?

2. Using Gould's explanation of NOMA, describe the relationship he sees between faith and reason (or scientific inquiry). Point out the similarities between the idea of NOMA and the statement from Saint John Paul II quoted in the introduction to this excerpt.

3. Can you name other conflicts between science and religion or faith and reason that can be solved by NOMA or by an understanding of the statement of Saint John Paul II?

21 A Community of the Faithful

Introduction

Elizabeth Johnson, professor of theology at Fordham University in New York City, quotes Simone Weil (see chapter 5, "Christ's Presence in the Church") concerning the need not just for saints today but also for saintliness. For Johnson, like Weil, saintliness may not look like the traditional form we have come to expect from the saints and martyrs in the past. For instance, Saint Ignatius of Antioch (see chapter 2, "Witness to Christ") may have suffered a horrific death in the Roman Coliseum, but his faith in the Risen Christ was clear and

> *Saints may not necessarily be persons who have found God; in fact, they may experience in a profound way the absence of God. Yet they try to walk with others faithfully even in the darkness and their restless hearts do not stop seeking.*

unambiguous. In a certain sense, living under persecution had the advantage of providing both sides with clearly defined roles. On one side there is the community of the faithful; on the other, the persecuting authority. A Christian either renounces faith in Christ or suffers the consequences. However, as Johnson points out, today we have experienced an "eclipse" of the divine, and so the former definition and clarity are lacking. A new kind of "holiness might well take the form of waiting determinedly and passionately for God. Saints may not necessarily be persons who have found God. . . . Yet they try to walk with others faithfully even in the darkness and their restless hearts do not stop seeking."

The example of holiness that Johnson cites in the following reading comes out of the tragic but sadly common experience of

> **Paschal Mystery**
>
> *Paschal* refers to the *pasch*, or Passover, in the Old Testament, and to Easter in the Gospels. The Paschal Mystery is the Passion-death-Resurrection-Ascension of Christ, solemnly celebrated during the Easter Triduum (from Holy Thursday evening to Easter Sunday evening) and made a present reality in every liturgical celebration.

domestic violence. As you read the story, note that saintliness is found not in extraordinary deeds or grand public acts but in living a simple, quiet life of holiness. What is holiness? It is the "slow process of spiritual growth" that enables a person to bear the trials of everyday life and not give up hope. It is not responding in kind to all of those things that belittle and humiliate and deny human worth. It is not giving in to despair when there is every reason to do so. It is having faith that God will not leave us, that we will suffer and grieve, laugh and give thanks all in the name of the one who is love. It is cherishing every moment of life not because it is good but because it is real.

The lives of the ordinary people Johnson mentions are certainly real, linked together in the great community of faith that includes the living, the dead who have died in Christ and still live in him, and those yet to be born. Of fundamental importance is bringing all of these saints into the present memory of the Church, which is what we do in the Eucharistic liturgy when we celebrate the Paschal Mystery of Christ. They are all present with us in that great, saving act of remembering. In the Eucharist we are united with all the saints and find the courage to follow in their footsteps.

Excerpt from *Friends of God and Prophets*
By Elizabeth A. Johnson

Creative fidelity in everyday life takes different forms in different eras. "Today, it is not nearly enough merely to be a saint, but we must have the saintliness demanded by the present moment, a new saintliness, itself also without precedent."[1] Simone Weil, who penned these lines, envisioned that in the modern age of divine eclipse, holiness might well take the form of waiting determinedly and passionately for God. Saints may not necessarily be persons who have found God; in fact, they may experience in a profound way the absence of God. Yet they try to walk with others faithfully even in the darkness and their restless hearts do not stop seeking. In Theresa Sanders's engaging view, this holiness entails not so much an accomplishment as being on fire with desire, saints being those whose hunger and thirst for God is insatiable.[2] In our day too, the arena for holy action stretches from the personal sphere to the farthest reaches of the political, with asceticism suffered not for its good effect on one's personal spiritual standing but as an inevitable by-product of struggling for the well-being of the dear neighbor. Religious attention shifts away from miraculous deeds that defy the laws of nature to deeds of friendship and prophecy that defy the weight of systemic power and privilege. Spiritual value is given to action on behalf of justice and against racism, sexism, classism; to endeavors of active nonviolent resistance for peace; to measures that promote meaning among the young and dignity among the old; to efforts to cultivate kinship with the earth and protect it from harm; to works of building communities of mutuality; and to acts of shucking off denigrating self-images, refusing victimization, blessing the body, finding one's voice, and speaking the truth in all boldness.

In an interesting thought experiment, Rembert Weakland invites us to imagine what such spiritual passion would look like in the year 2100. His candidate for sainthood is one Ellen Piasecki, married, mother of three children, worker in a local brewery, accidentally killed at the age of forty-five when she was called out to help a neighbor being brutalized by domestic violence. She had already wrestled with the vagaries of life, including breast cancer and the stresses of an unemployed husband. But through a slow process of spiritual growth fed by the Scriptures, the sacraments, and relationships with her family, co-workers, and other people, especially the poor, she became a deeply peaceful person rooted in God. Through an almost imperceptible process of maturing, she was purified from childhood expectations:

She did not seek a God of magic, a *deus ex machina* that could be turned off and on as needed, nor a schoolmaster to discipline society, nor a policeman to keep it in line, but she came to seek rather a God who was a lover, a friend, a transcendent other—bigger than she but not distant from her. Once she had discovered that God was a companion, she seemed able to relax in that transcendent presence that was so real and so close to her.[3]

No goody-goody, she worked on her relationship with her husband and reared her children with the usual ups and downs. Her family, co-workers, fellow parishioners, and citizens of Milwaukee, where she served on a reconciliation commission, found her more and more to be a caring woman with a listening ear, a compassionate heart, and a passion for peacemaking, not taken with herself but radiating a spiritual depth that was crucial to their own growth in faith. In the end, she protected a wife and kids from a raging husband, becoming caught in the crossfire herself. In this typically American midwestern setting, Ellen was an example in death as in life: "she mirrored Christ to us . . . taught us how to relate to God in a new way . . . how to be a practitioner of peace like Jesus," and one hundred years later her memory continues to inspire. Yes, Weakland concludes, her goodness and giftedness became famous because of the notoriety surrounding her death. But "how many others are there out there who do not become famous?"[4] . . .

3. Cloud of Witnesses through Time

The communion of saints is not restricted to persons who live and breathe at the present moment, but embraces those who have gone through the shattering of death into eternal life. Only the hope that God is trustworthy can ground this interpretation, for death truly ends life as we know it. What follows is unimaginable, and no pictorial description of saints in heaven is ever remotely adequate. What Christian faith affirms of persons who lived and died trying to respond to the Spirit, even in their failure, is simply and radically this: *Vivit! [He / she lives!]*—by the mercy of God. As George Tavard has succinctly written, this "is not the fruit of works or the reward of individual merit, but it is entirely God's gift. All the faithful on earth are saints in the biblical sense of the term. All those who die in Christ are saints in heaven."[5] And both groups are linked by their communion with the living God who pervades and transcends the boundaries of time itself.

The company of saints in heaven beggars description. While some few are remembered by name, it enfolds millions upon anonymous millions of people whom we will never know. In different times and places their imagination and initiatives brought compassion alive in their own corner of life and comforted, healed, and challenged the world in ways that we can never imagine. "By passing along the narrow road they widened it, and while they went along, trampling on the rough ways, they went ahead of us,"[6] as Augustine preached. Their pioneering faith, replete with hope in divine mercy over sinfulness, and the patterns of goodness they traced in history make our life possible. Bearers of our past, they also signify our future.

Among these saints, known and mostly unknown, are counted those untimely dead, killed in godforsaken incidents of terror, war, and mass death, their life's projects cut down in mid-stride. Having drunk so deeply of the cup of crucifixion, they call forth special mention in anguish and lament. Among these saints are also numbered some whom we knew personally. Their number increases as we get older: grandparents, mother and father, sisters and brothers, beloved spouses and life partners, children, teachers, students, patients, clients, friends and colleagues, relatives and neighbors, spiritual guides and religious leaders. Their good lives, complete with fault and failure, have reached journey's end. Gone from us, they have arrived home in unspeakable, unimaginable life within the embrace of God. To say of all these people that they form with us the company of the redeemed is to give grief a direction, affirming that in the dialogue between God and the human race the last word is the gracious word of life. In instances where persons have wrought real and lasting damage by their actions, faith holds out the possibility that at their deepest core they did not concur in diabolical evil. The church's prayer is that God will be more merciful toward them than they have been to others. On their behalf, at least we may hope.

Cheered on by this great, richly varied cloud of witnesses, learning their "lessons of encouragement,"[7] protesting their pain, catching their hope, standing on their shoulders, the church today takes its own steps on the path of discipleship as legacy for future generations. Orthodox theologian Kallistos Ware spins out a beautiful metaphor of this relationship when he writes, "The saints in each generation, joined to those who have gone before, and filled like them with light, become a golden chain in which each saint is a separate link, united to the next by faith, works, and love. So in the One God they form a single chain which cannot quickly be broken."[8]

Saints on earth have access to the company of saints in heaven through memory and hope. Memory is meant here in the sense of *anamnesis,* an effective remembering that makes something genuinely past to be present and active in the community today. A remembered event becomes a living force in history when it is recalled and narrated; in the very retelling power comes forth to change the horizon of our days and offer new possibilities of existence. The primary *anamnesis* of the Christian community occurs in the sacramental action of the Eucharist, where the community makes memorial of Jesus' death and resurrection in such a way that it becomes a living, transforming reality in the lives of those who celebrate it.[9] Christian remembrance of the saints is linked to this action, making present the creative struggle and witness of so many who themselves participated in this paschal mystery. Retelling their story brings the subversive, encouraging, and liberating power of their love and witness into the present generation.

Endnotes

1. Simone Weil, *Waiting for God*, trans. Emma Craufurd (New York: Putnam, 1951), 99.
2. Theresa Sanders, "Seeking a Minor Sun: Saints after the Death of God," *Horizons: Journal of the College Theology Society* 22 (1995): 183–97.
3. Georgia Harkness, *Our Christian Hope* (New York: Abingdon Press, 1964), 54. Writing in the same vein, Dietrich Bonhoeffer affirms that this is the church's hope which it guards like a treasure: *The Communion of Saints*, trans. R. Gregor Smith (New York: Harper & Row, 1963), 199–202.
4. Rahner, "The Eternal Significance of the Humanity of Jesus," 36; see also J. Gerald Janzen, "Modes of Presence and the Communion of Saints," in *Religious Experience and Process Theology*, eds. Harry James Cargas and Bernard Lee (New York: Paulist, 1976), 147–72.
5. Karl Rahner, "The Life of the Dead," *Theological Investigations* 4:353–54; see also his "Hidden Victory," *Theological Investigations* 7 (New York: Seabury, 1977), 151–58; and "Experiencing Easter," *Theological Investigations* 7:159–68.

6. Mic 6:8.

7. See Edward Farley's analysis of hope as a word of power in need of new retrieval in *Deep Symbols,* 95–112 . . . ; and Karl Rahner, "On the Theology of Hope," *Theological Investigations* 10:242–59, and "Faith as Courage," *Theological Investigations* 18, trans. Edward Quinn (New York: Crossroad, 1983), 211–25.

8. Quoted in Jon Sobrino, *Jesus in Latin America* (Maryknoll, N.Y.: Orbis, 1987), 96–97; I am indebted to Melanie May for this interpretation. For the way hope functions creatively as a counterweight to evil in the lives of the poor, see Jon Sobrino, "Evil and Hope: A Reflection from the Victims," trans. Orlando Espín, *Catholic Theological Society of America Proceedings* 50 (1995):71–84, with response by Maria Pílar Aquino, 85–92.

9. McFague, *The Body of God,* 202.

For Reflection

1. According to Johnson, saintliness is not about "miraculous deeds that defy the laws of nature" but actions on behalf of the oppressed. Do you agree? Explain your answer.

2. Do you agree with Rembert Weakland's choice of Ellen Piasecki as a candidate for sainthood? Why or why not?

3. Discuss the similarities and differences between Saint Ignatius of Antioch and Ellen Piasecki.

4. What "patterns of goodness" can you identify in your own life? Where are they found?

22 Cheap Grace and Costly Grace

Introduction

Among the many themes that have emerged from the readings, two are clear: persecution for the faith and putting that faith into action in the everyday world. These come together in the life of Dietrich Bonhoeffer (1906–1945), a German Lutheran pastor who understood that for faith in Christ to mean anything, it must be lived, especially under trying circumstances. The circumstances that tried, even threatened, his faith were **National Socialism** and World War II.

Bonhoeffer was part of a group of theologians and church leaders opposed to Hitler and the German Church's support of Nazi policies, which these churchmen determined were not only ungodly but inhuman. Bonhoeffer felt that the official German Church had sold out to Hitler to protect itself and its status in society. He believed that if Christians were to be true to their faith, they would have to stand with Christ in the good times and the bad, when it was popular to do so and not so popular. In the end Bonhoeffer lost his life for standing with Christ. In 1945 two years after being arrested by the Gestapo for treason against Hitler, Bonhoeffer was hanged at Flossenburg concentration camp. Sadly, this was just days before the Allies liberated Flossenburg.

National Socialism The official name for Adolf Hitler's political movement and party. The party was built on a philosophy of centralized government, unfailing allegiance to *der Führer* ("the leader"), a professional military, the genetic superiority of the German people, and *Lebensraum*, or the right to conquer needed territory. Followers of National Socialism were popularly known as "Nazis."

In the essay that follows, Bonhoeffer distinguishes between two worlds, not unlike Saint Augustine's comparison of the City of God to the City of the World. Bonhoeffer's worlds are "cheap grace" and "costly grace." The former is relatively easy. It is knowing the right things to say and providing the correct answers as to what constitutes a Christian life. A good Christian goes to church, follows the Commandments, does well in school, and stays true to a sweetheart. These are all fine things in themselves, but Bonhoeffer says they don't make us Christian. They provide us with cheap grace, which allows us the leisure of hypocrisy so that we feel good about ourselves. We end up asking for forgiveness without being repentant, putting two dollars in the collection but spending two hundred on jeans, going to Communion on Sunday but slandering friends on Monday morning. Costly grace, on the other hand, is doing the unpopular thing like admitting wrongdoing, giving money not out of charity but from the heart, and defending those people deemed to be "uncool." This is why grace costs us something, and, even though God freely offers grace, it is still a struggle to accept his gift and live it out faithfully.

Finally, as we learn from this excerpt, costly grace has to be renewed continually, sometimes daily, which means it requires a commitment. Sometimes we fail in that commitment, but we must not let ourselves be discouraged or give up because of failure. There is always tomorrow and the day after to renew the grace that demands that we be real. Bonhoeffer reminds us that, for Christians, few things are worse than living a life of cheap grace but nothing grander than the freedom of the grace that costs.

Excerpt from *The Cost of Discipleship*
By Dietrich Bonhoeffer

Chapter 1: Costly Grace

CHEAP GRACE is the deadly enemy of our Church. We are fighting today for costly grace.

cheapjacks Peddlers of shoddy goods.

Cheap grace means grace sold on the market like **cheapjacks'** wares. The sacraments, the forgiveness of sin, and the consolations of religion are thrown away at cut prices. Grace is represented as the Church's inexhaustible treasury, from which she showers blessings with generous hands, without asking questions or fixing limits. Grace without price; grace without cost! The essence of grace, we suppose, is that the account has been paid in advance; and, because it has been paid, everything can be had for nothing. Since the cost was infinite, the possibilities of using and spending it are infinite. What would grace be if it were not cheap?

Cheap grace means grace as a doctrine, a principle, a system. It means forgiveness of sins proclaimed as a general truth, the love of God taught as the Christian "conception" of God. An intellectual assent to that idea is held to be of itself sufficient to secure remission of sins. The Church which holds the correct doctrine of grace has, it is supposed, *ipso facto* a part in that grace. In such a Church the world finds a cheap covering for its sins; no contrition is required, still less any real desire to be delivered from sin. Cheap grace therefore amounts to a denial of the living Word of God, in fact, a denial of the Incarnation of the Word of God.

Luther (1483–1546)

Martin Luther was originally a Catholic Augustinian monk. His famous Ninety-Five Theses (1517) set in motion the Protestant Reformation. He criticized the primacy of the Pope, papal infallibility, the sacrifice of the Mass, and many Church practices of the sixteenth century. He developed a distinct understanding of justification based on Romans 1:16–17 (see chapter 14, "Second Mark: The Church Is Holy").

Cheap grace means the justification of sin without the justification of the sinner. Grace alone does everything, they say, and so everything can remain as it was before. "All for sin could not atone." The world goes on in the same old way, and we are still sinners "even in the best life" as Luther said. Well, then, let the Christian live like the rest of the world, let him model himself on the world's standards in every sphere of life, and not presumptuously aspire to live a different life under grace from his old life under sin.

That was the heresy of the enthusi-asts, the Anabaptists and their kind. Let the Christian beware of rebelling against the free and boundless grace of God and desecrating it. Let him not attempt to erect a new religion of the letter by endeavouring to live a life of obedience to the commandments of Jesus Christ! The world has been justified by grace. The Christian knows that, and takes it seriously. He knows he must not strive against this indispensable grace. Therefore—let him live like the rest of the world! Of course he would like to go and do something extraordinary, and it does demand a

> **Anabaptists**
>
> This term for a particular group of Christian believers was taken from the Greek to "rebaptize," based on a rejection of infant Baptism in favor of a "baptism of believers." Thus one must be baptized as an adult to give meaning and credibility to the commitment to Jesus Christ. The term refers to a number of various Christian groups throughout Europe that emerged in the sixteenth century. In the United States, they are chiefly known as Hutterites.

good deal of self-restraint to refrain from the attempt and content himself with living as the world lives. Yet it is imperative for the Christian to achieve renunciation, to practise self-effacement, to distinguish his life from the life of the world. He must let grace be grace indeed, otherwise he will destroy the world's faith in the free gift of grace. Let the Christian rest content with his worldliness and with this renunciation of any higher standard than the world. He is doing it for the sake of the world rather than for the sake of grace. Let him be comforted and rest assured in his possession of this grace—for grace alone does everything. Instead of following Christ, let the Christian enjoy the consolations of his grace! That is what we mean by cheap grace, the grace which amounts to the justification of sin without the justification of the repentant sinner who departs from sin and from whom sin departs. Cheap grace is not the kind of forgiveness of sin which frees us from the toils of sin. Cheap grace is the grace we bestow on ourselves.

Cheap grace is the preaching of forgiveness without requiring repentance, baptism without church discipline, Communion without confession, absolution without personal confession. Cheap grace is grace without discipleship, grace without the cross, grace without Jesus Christ, living and incarnate.

Costly grace is the treasure hidden in the field; for the sake of it a man will gladly go and sell all that he has. It is the pearl of great price to buy which the merchant will sell all his goods. It is the kingly rule of Christ, for whose sake a man will pluck out the eye which causes him to stumble, it is the call of Jesus Christ at which the disciple leaves his nets and follows him.

Costly grace is the gospel which must be *sought* again and again, the gift which must be *asked* for, the door at which a man must *knock.*

Such grace is *costly* because it calls us to follow, and it is *grace* because it calls us to follow *Jesus Christ.* It is costly because it costs a man his life, and it is grace because it gives a man the only true life. It is costly because it condemns sin, and grace because it justifies the sinner. Above

> " *Costly grace confronts us as a gracious call to follow Jesus, it comes as a word of forgiveness to the broken spirit and the contrite heart. Grace is costly because it compels a man to submit to the yoke of Christ and follow him.* "

all, it is *costly* because it cost God the life of his Son: "ye were bought at a price," and what has cost God much cannot be cheap for us. Above all, it is *grace* because God did not reckon his Son too dear a price to pay for our life, but delivered him up for us. Costly grace is the Incarnation of God.

Costly grace is the sanctuary of God; it has to be protected from the world, and not thrown to the dogs. It is therefore the living word, the Word of God, which he speaks as it pleases him. Costly grace confronts us as a gracious call to follow Jesus, it comes as a word of forgiveness to the broken spirit and the contrite heart. Grace is costly because it compels a man to submit to the yoke of Christ and follow him; it is grace because Jesus says: "My yoke is easy and my burden is light."

On two separate occasions Peter received the call, "Follow me." It was the first and last word Jesus spoke to his disciple (Mark 1.17; John 21.22). A whole life lies between these two calls. The first occasion was by the lake of Gennesareth, when Peter left his nets and his craft and followed Jesus at his word. The second occasion is when the Risen Lord finds him back again at his old trade. Once again it is by the lake of Gennesareth, and once again the call is: "Follow me." Between the two calls lay a whole life of discipleship in the following of Christ. Half-way between them comes Peter's confession, when he acknowledged Jesus as the Christ of God. Three times Peter hears the same proclamation that Christ is his Lord and God—at the beginning, at the end, and at Caesarea Philippi. Each time it is the same grace of Christ which calls to him "Follow me" and which reveals itself to him in his confession of the Son of God. Three times on Peter's way did grace arrest him, the one grace proclaimed in three different ways.

This grace was certainly not self-bestowed. It was the grace of Christ himself, now prevailing upon the disciple to leave all and follow him, now working in him that confession which to the world must sound like the ultimate blasphemy, now inviting Peter to the supreme fellowship of martyrdom for the Lord he had denied, and thereby forgiving him all his sins. In the life of Peter grace and discipleship are inseparable. He had received the grace which costs.

For Reflection

1. Apply Bonhoeffer's distinction between cheap grace and costly grace to your own life. Where do you see each at work?

2. Do you think Bonhoeffer's call to live a life of costly grace is too idealistic or unattainable? Why or why not?

3. Bonhoeffer alludes to the Matthean parable (see Matthew 13:45–46) of the "pearl of great price." What is your pearl of great price?

4. Bonhoeffer's "cheap grace" can also be called "hypocrisy." Where in society today, or in your life or in the lives of teens today, might you find hypocrisy?

Part 5

Implications for the Life of the Believer

23 Breakthrough to God

Introduction

So far, you have read excerpts related to different themes, including persecution, mystery, and paradox in the Christian faith. To these, with Meister Eckhart (1260–1327), we add breakthrough. Eckhart was a Dominican monk and professor of theology at the University of Paris, the same university where Thomas Aquinas (see chapter 12, "'A Tower of Refuge'") taught. Through his work in his native Germany and France, Eckhart became interested in the question of God's grace and where it might be found. That is, how do we get so close to God that we not only experience God's love but also become one with him, as Jesus exhorts us to do in John 17:21–23? Martin Luther asked the same question two hundred years later and found his answer in Romans 1:16–17, which was the basis for his theology of justification by faith (see chapter 22 sidebar "Luther"). Eckhart followed a more mystical path in which the individual has to break through (*durchbrechen*) barriers of thought, will, and desire (i.e., the ego) to get to the inner ground of God, *der Grunt*.

detachment In Eckhart's view, spiritual poverty that renounces not only material things but also one's own intellectual concepts about God.

apophatic theology So-called negative theology, which holds that we can really approach God only through discernment and prayer, not through intellectual concepts. Eckhart's theology and spirituality are apophatic.

How does one do this? Eckhart believed that by becoming poor in spirit, a Christian could break through the ego to fathom the depths of God, but he recognized that this is an arduous process fraught with challenges. His description of the process is sometimes hard to follow, for he called for a transformation in the way we view spiritual poverty. Central to his thinking was the necessity of **detachment**. For instance, he wrote that to meet God, we must be free of all material things that weigh us down: "You must know that to be empty of all created things is to be full of God, and to be full of created things is to be empty of God." In addition, not only must the ego be stripped through detachment, but all expectations about God's will must be abandoned. Eckhart was convinced that this was necessary to encounter God and become one with the Divine in a creature-Creator relationship. "Nakedness" is an important element in this process, for, as the editors of a compilation of Eckhart's essays explain, "the greater the nakedness, the greater the union." By *nakedness*, Eckhart means the psychic-spiritual nakedness of giving oneself completely to another, to God.

> **The Inquisitions**
>
> The Medieval Inquisition was a Church tribunal established by the Pope in 1231 to deal with heresy, or the rejection of official Church teaching. Verdicts were enforced by secular rulers and the Inquisitors, who came from the Dominican and Franciscan orders. The Spanish Inquisition, begun about two hundred years later (1481), was organized by the king and queen of Spain (Ferdinand II and Isabella) and was not conducted under official Church authority.

In the following excerpt from *Sermon 52,* you will read Eckhart's view of spiritual poverty in which he describes emptying the self in order to be filled not with God but with nothing. Why? Because in this way, "if God wishes to work in the soul, he himself is the place in which he wants to work." Eckhart taught that the individual must give up all preconceived ideas and notions of who and what God is (a negative theology, or **apophatic theology**). Once this is achieved, the Christian will be able to become one with the Father, just as Jesus and the Father were one. This teaching eventually got Eckhart into trouble with the Inquisition, and several of his teachings were condemned after his death. Today, however, his contributions to the spiritual life of Christians and to the Catholic Church are recognized as both valid and valuable.

Why would Eckhart's negative theology be important for us today? Through Eckhart's theology, we learn humility—the truth of who we are and who God is. We know that in Jesus Christ, God has revealed himself to us to the fullest extent possible. Yet, where God is concerned, mystery remains. We find glimpses of God everywhere, yet no one can be a "know-it-all" about God—until we meet him face-to-face in Heaven (see 1 Corinthians 13:12).

Excerpt from *Sermon 52*
By Meister Eckhart

I have said just now that a man is poor who does not want to fulfill God's will, but who lives so that he may be free both of his own will and of God's will, as he was when he was not. About this poverty I say that it is the highest poverty. Second, I say that a man is poor who knows nothing of God's works in him. A man who is so established is as free of knowing and perceiving as God is free of all things, and this is the purest poverty. But a third form is the most intimate poverty, on which I now want to speak; and this is when a man has nothing.

Now pay great attention and give heed! I have often said, and great authorities say, that a man should be so free of all things and of all works, both interior and exterior, that he might become a place only for God in which God could work. Now I say otherwise. If it be the case that man is free of all created things and of God himself and if it also be that God may find place in him in which to work, then I say that so long as that is in man, he is not poor with the most intimate poverty. For it is not God's intention in his works that man should have in himself a place for God to work in. Poverty of spirit is for a man to keep so free of God and of all his works that if God wishes to work in the soul, he himself is the place in which he wants to work; and that he will gladly do. For if he finds a man so poor as this, then God performs his own work, and the man is in this way suffering [allowing] God to work, and God is his own place to work in, and so God is his own worker in himself. Thus in this poverty man pursues that everlasting being which he was and which he is now and which he will evermore remain.

It is Saint Paul who says: "All that I am, I am by God's grace" (1 Co. 15:10). But if what I say, "transcends grace and being and understanding and will and longing," how then can Paul's words be true? People show that what Paul said is true in this way. That the grace of God was in him was necessarily so, for it was God's grace working in him that brought what was accidental to the perfection of the essential. When grace had finished and had perfected its work, then Paul remained what he was.

So I say that man should be so poor that he should not be or have any place in which God could work. When man clings to place, he clings to distinction. Therefore I pray to God that he may make me free of "God," for my real being is above God if we take "God" to be the beginning of created things. For in the same being of God where God is above being and above distinction, there I myself was, there I willed myself and committed myself to create this man. Therefore I am the cause of myself in the order of my being, which is eternal, and not in the order of my becoming, which is temporal. And therefore I am unborn, and in the manner in which I am unborn I can never die. In my unborn manner I have been eternally, and am now, and shall eternally remain. What I am in the order of having been born, that will die and perish, for it is mortal, and so it must in time suffer corruption. In my birth all things were born and I was the cause of myself and of all things; and if I would have wished it, I would not be nor would all other things be. And if I did not exist, "God" would also not exist. That God is "God," of that I am a cause; if I did not exist, God too would not be "God." There is no need to understand this.

A great authority says that his breaking through is nobler than his flowing out;[1] and that is true. When I flowed out from God, all things said: "God is." And this cannot make me blessed, for with this I acknowledge that I am a creature. But in the breaking-through, when I come to be free of will of myself and of God's will and of all his works and of God himself, then I am above all created things, and I am neither God nor creature, but I am what I was and what I shall remain, now and eternally. Then I received an impulse that will bring me up above all the angels.

Together with this impulse, I receive such riches that God, as he is "God," and as he performs all his divine works, cannot suffice me; for in this breaking-through I receive that God and I are one. Then I am what I was, and then I neither diminish nor increase, for I am then an immovable cause that moves all things. Here God finds no place in man, for with this poverty man achieves what he has been eternally and will evermore remain. Here God is one with the spirit, and that is the most intimate poverty one can find.

> " *Here God is one with the spirit, and that is the most intimate poverty one can find.* "

Whoever does not understand what I have said, let him not burden his heart with it; for as long as a man is not equal to this truth, he will not understand these words, for this is a truth beyond speculation that has come immediately from the heart of God. May God help us so to live that we may find it eternally. Amen.

Endnote

1. Some suggest that the "great authority" is Eckhart himself.

For Reflection

1. How might one achieve "poverty of spirit" in Eckhart's understanding of the term?

2. Why does Eckhart pray to be "free of 'God'"?

3. Do you find Eckhart's spirituality appealing? Why or why not?

4. How might Eckhart's approach to grace and his emphasis on detachment influence a person's interaction with the world today?

24 Plumbing the Depths: *Duc in Altum!*

Introduction

The expression *duc in altum,* Latin for "go into the deep," comes from Pope Saint John Paul II's Apostolic Letter *Novo Millennio Ineunte* ("At the Close of the Great Jubilee of the Year 2000"). The Pope wrote it to commemorate the two thousandth anniversary of the birth of Christ and to set a new tone for the Church, one marked by sincere devotion and "fresh enthusiasm" to follow Christ by deeds, as well as words. The expression "go into the deep" is taken from Luke 5:4. In this account Simon Peter and the other disciples have been fishing all night but come up with nothing, their nets empty. Jesus tells them to set out again into the deep water. Reluctantly they do, and catch so many fish that "their nets were tearing" (Luke 5:6). This story is significant for discipleship in two ways. First, it teaches us that with God nothing is impossible, even those things—*especially* those things—that to us seem beyond hope. Second, it reminds us to think big when it comes to faith and reminds us

> **Jubilee Year**
>
> The Jubilee Year is celebrated in the Catholic Church every 50 years. It is a year of rededication to Jesus Christ and to the living of the Gospel. The last Jubilee Year was the year 2000. The custom of the Jubilee Year has its roots in the Israelite custom of celebrating the conclusion of "seven weeks of years" (seven weeks multiplied by seven days per week equal 49 years), with a year of "jubilee," in which all debt was forgiven, prisoners were released from captivity, slaves were freed, and servants were allowed to return home. For the Israelites, the custom was similar to God resting on the seventh day (see Leviticus, chapter 25).

that individuals and the world can be changed with the grace of God and belief in the redeeming act of the cross.

Saint John Paul's call to go into the deep is also significant in that it asks all Christians, not just professional ministers or the clergy, to take on the task of evangelization, which is proclaiming the Word of God by what we say and how we live, to other people and cultures, even our own. He has asked all of us to be part of the Church's effort to engage the world in a way that will help it encounter the Risen Christ and his promise that no one ever need fear again. If the world says there is no God or asks where God is and why he is hidden, as disciples we answer that God is not hidden but revealed in the one crucified for us so that we may live. Thus going into the deep requires that we be aware of the cross and its symbolic meaning, not only of the Christian mystery but of ultimate life.

The following excerpts come from different sections of *Novo Millennio Ineunte*. In the first (30–31), the Pope refers to a document from Vatican Council II that you have already encountered, *Lumen Gentium* (see chapter 9, "A Church in Exile"). He uses it to speak of holiness, which, like evangelization, affects all Christians. In other words, holiness is not just for saints or those with a particular charism but is rather the goal of all Christians. He contrasts this with settling for a "life of mediocrity." In the second section (40–41), he talks about the "new evangelization" directed to people in the developed world and how it too is everyone's task. In summary, what this document and excerpt ask of us is to live a real life, not a half-hearted one, and to be real when it comes to our faith. If we believe that Christ actually rose from the dead and that he offers us life, why be afraid of anything? Live deep, go deep!

Excerpt from "Apostolic Letter *Novo Millennio Ineunte* of His Holiness Pope John Paul II"

By Pope Saint John Paul II

Holiness

30. First of all, I have no hesitation in saying that all pastoral initiatives must be set in relation to *holiness*. Was this not the ultimate meaning of the Jubilee indulgence, as a special grace offered by Christ so that the life of every baptized person could be purified and deeply renewed?

It is my hope that, among those who have taken part in the Jubilee, many will have benefited from this grace, in full awareness of its demands. Once the Jubilee is over, we resume our normal path, but knowing that stressing holiness remains more than ever an urgent pastoral task.

It is necessary therefore to rediscover the full practical significance of Chapter 5 of the Dogmatic Constitution on the Church *Lumen Gentium*, dedicated to the "universal call to holiness." The Council Fathers laid such stress on this point, not just to embellish ecclesiology with a kind of spiritual veneer, but to make the call to holiness an intrinsic and essential aspect of their teaching on the Church. The rediscovery of the Church as "mystery," or as a people "gathered together by the unity of the Father, the Son and the Holy Spirit,"[1] was bound to bring with it a rediscovery of the Church's "holiness," understood in the basic sense of belonging to him who is in essence the Holy One, the "thrice Holy" (cf. *Is* 6:3). To profess the Church as holy means to point to her as *the Bride of Christ,* for whom he gave himself precisely in order to make her holy (cf. *Eph* 5:25–26). This as it were objective gift of holiness is offered to all the baptized.

But the gift in turn becomes a task, which must shape the whole of Christian life: "This is the will of God, your sanctification" (*1 Th* 4:3). It is a duty which concerns not only certain Christians: "All the Christian faithful, of whatever state or rank, are called to the fullness of the Christian life and to the perfection of charity."[2]

31. At first glance, it might seem almost impractical to recall this elementary truth as the foundation of the pastoral planning in which

we are involved at the start of the new millennium. Can holiness ever be "planned"? What might the word "holiness" mean in the context of a pastoral plan?

In fact, to place pastoral planning under the heading of holiness is a choice filled with consequences. It implies the conviction that, since Baptism is a true entry into the holiness of God through incorporation into Christ and the indwelling of his Spirit, it would be a contradiction to settle for a life of mediocrity, marked by a minimalist ethic and a shallow religiosity. To ask catechumens: "Do you wish to receive Baptism?" means at the same time to ask them: "Do you wish to become holy?" It means to set before them the radical nature of the Sermon on the Mount: "Be perfect as your heavenly Father is perfect" (*Mt* 5:48).

As the Council itself explained, this ideal of perfection must not be misunderstood as if it involved some kind of extraordinary existence, possible only for a few "uncommon heroes" of holiness. The ways of holiness are many, according to the vocation of each individual. I thank the Lord that in these years he has enabled me to beatify and canonize a large number of Christians, and among them many lay people who attained holiness in the most ordinary circumstances of life. The time has come to re-propose wholeheartedly to everyone this *high standard of ordinary Christian living*: the whole life of the Christian community and of Christian families must lead in this direction. It is also clear however that the paths to holiness are personal and call for a genuine "*training in holiness,*" adapted to people's needs. This training must integrate the resources offered to everyone with both the traditional forms of individual and group assistance, as well as the more recent forms of support offered in associations and movements recognized by the Church.

Proclaiming the Word

40. To nourish ourselves with the word in order to be "servants of the word" in the work of evangelization: this is surely a priority for the Church at the dawn of the new millennium. Even in countries evangelized many centuries ago, the reality of a "Christian society" which, amid all the frailties which have always marked human life, measured itself explicitly on Gospel values, is now gone. Today we must courageously face

a situation which is becoming increasingly diversified and demanding, in the context of "globalization" and of the consequent new and uncertain mingling of peoples and cultures. Over the years, I have often repeated the summons to the *new evangelization.* I do so again now, especially in order to insist that we must rekindle in ourselves the impetus of the beginnings and allow ourselves to be filled with the ardour of the apostolic preaching which followed Pentecost. We must revive in ourselves the burning conviction of Paul, who cried out: "Woe to me if I do not preach the Gospel" (*1 Cor* 9:16).

> 66 *Those who have come into genuine contact with Christ cannot keep him for themselves, they must proclaim him.* 99

This passion will not fail to stir in the Church a new sense of mission, which cannot be left to a group of "specialists" but must involve the responsibility of all the members of the People of God. Those who have come into genuine contact with Christ cannot keep him for themselves, they must proclaim him. A new apostolic outreach is needed, which will be lived as *the everyday commitment of Christian communities and groups.* This should be done however with the respect due to the different paths of different people and with sensitivity to the diversity of cultures in which the Christian message must be planted, in such a way that the particular values of each people will not be rejected but purified and brought to their fullness.

In the Third Millennium, Christianity will have to respond ever more effectively to this *need for inculturation.* Christianity, while remaining completely true to itself, with unswerving fidelity to the proclamation of the Gospel and the tradition of the Church, will also reflect the different faces of the cultures and peoples in which it is received and takes root. In this Jubilee Year, we have rejoiced in a special way in the beauty of the Church's varied face. This is perhaps only a beginning, a barely sketched image of the future which the Spirit of God is preparing for us.

Christ must be presented to all people with confidence. We shall address adults, families, young people, children, without ever hiding the most radical demands of the Gospel message, but taking into account each

Sanguis martyrum semen christiano-rum. "The blood of the martyrs is the seed of Christians" (Tertullian). The Church has survived two millennia through the witness of its members, some of whom (the martyrs) have given their blood.

person's needs in regard to their sensitivity and language, after the example of Paul who declared: "I have become all things to all men, that I might by all means save some" (*1 Cor* 9:22). In making these recommendations, I am thinking especially of *the pastoral care of young people*. Precisely in regard to young people, as I said earlier, the Jubilee has given us an encouraging testimony of their generous availability. We must learn to interpret that heartening response, by investing that enthusiasm like a new talent (cf. *Mt* 25:15) which the Lord has put into our hands so that we can make it yield a rich return.

41. May the shining example of the many witnesses to the faith whom we have remembered during the Jubilee sustain and guide us in this confident, enterprising and creative sense of mission. For the Church, the martyrs have always been a seed of life. ***Sanguis martyrum semen christianorum:***[3] this famous "law" formulated by Tertullian has proved true in all the trials of history. Will this not also be the case of the century and millennium now beginning? Perhaps we were too used to thinking of the martyrs in rather distant terms, as though they were a category of the past, associated especially with the first centuries of the Christian era. The Jubilee remembrance has presented us with a surprising vista, showing us that our own time is particularly prolific in witnesses, who in different ways were able to live the Gospel in the midst of hostility and persecution, often to the point of the supreme test of shedding their blood. In them the word of God, sown in good soil, yielded a hundred fold (cf. *Mt* 13:8, 23). By their example they have shown us, and made smooth for us, so to speak, the path to the future. All that remains for us is, with God's grace, to follow in their footsteps.

Endnotes

1. Saint Cyprian, *De Oratione Dominica,* 23: *PL* 4, 553; cf. *Lumen Gentium,* 4.
2. Second Vatican Ecumenical Council, Dogmatic Constitution on the Church *Lumen Gentium,* 40.
3. Tertullian, *Apologeticum,* 50, 13: *PL* 1, 534.

For Reflection

1. Contrast holiness with mediocrity in your life.

2. How might you take part in the new evangelization?

3. Discuss how trials and persecutions have enriched the Church.

4. How would you answer Pope Saint John Paul II's question to the catechumens, "Do you wish to become holy?"

25 Living Liturgically

Introduction

Only ninety-five pages in its English translation, *The Spirit of the Liturgy,* by Romano Guardini (1885–1968), has been considered a masterpiece of liturgical theology and spiritual writing since its original German-language publication in 1918. For nearly one hundred years, it has provided remarkable insight into the nature of worship and sound theological advice for participating in the liturgy and living liturgically beyond Sunday. Guardini, who was a priest, a professor, and what we would call today a "youth minister," tells his readers that the essence of the liturgy is humility, which is needed to encounter God and to discipline oneself to participate fully in the assembly. The fruit of the liturgy, cultivated over years of attending Mass and participating in the ritual life of the Church, is courage. Those who live liturgically, Guardini says, find "peace to the depths of their being" and become men and women of courage. Because he was subject to bouts of depression from his youth, Guardini wrote from personal experience. What, then, is required to live liturgically? One must empty oneself to be filled with God's abiding presence in the ritual. Once that occurs, it is a natural step to living peacefully and courageously outside of Mass.

If you have ever found yourself thinking that Mass is boring, that going to church is a waste of time, or that you get nothing out of the liturgy, Guardini has an answer for you. First, he believed that what makes Mass boring is not the repetitive ritual acts that seem to make no sense and are unrelated to the world outside of Mass but rather our own inability to be quiet and to enter into our inner lives, our spiritual selves, to find God there, closer to us than we are to ourselves. Second, yes, church is a waste of time, as it should be. "The soul," he writes, "must learn to abandon, at least in prayer, the restlessness of purposeful activity; it must learn to waste time for the sake of God." His view of the human condition is summed up in his opposition to the idea that humans must always be rushing around somewhere for some purpose or for some reason. That kind of attitude actually makes us *less* human, because in our pursuit to get things done, we have little time left over for what really matters: relationships. As for getting nothing out of the liturgy, one must have the ears to hear and the eyes to see in order to get something out of anything. That means it is up to us to change. In addition, liturgy is worship, not entertainment or even education. We gather to give thanks and praise to the Creator, in the name of Christ through the Holy Spirit.

As you read the following excerpt, pay particular attention to what Guardini says about the purposelessness of the liturgy, play, freedom, and the mental discipline necessary to enter into the liturgy and to live liturgically. What kind of world is he describing? A spirituality is also present in his writing; one might identify it as a liturgical spirituality. The essence of such a spirituality is that along with bread and wine becoming the Body and Blood of Christ in the Eucharist, we too turn from flesh and bone into the living Body of Christ.

Excerpt from *The Spirit of the Liturgy*
By Romano Guardini

Of course, it can be said of the liturgy, as of every action and every prayer which it contains, that it is directed towards the providing of spiritual instruction. This is perfectly true. But the liturgy has no thought-out, deliberate, detailed plan of instruction. In order to sense the difference it is sufficient to compare a week of the ecclesiastical year with the Spiritual Exercises of St. Ignatius. In the latter every element is determined by deliberate choice, everything is directed towards the production of a certain spiritual and **didactic**

didactic From the Greek, meaning "intended to teach."

Spiritual Exercises of Saint Ignatius

These are a set of exercises done over the course of thirty days to deepen one's commitment to Jesus Christ through discernment of God's will. As Guardini explains, these exercises are structured, intentional, and deliberate. A retreatant follows a program of prayer and reflection based on the life and ministry of Jesus; his death, Resurrection, and Ascension; the coming of the Holy Spirit at Pentecost; and the work of the Holy Spirit in the world today.

result; each exercise, each prayer, even the way in which the hours of repose are passed, all aim at the one thing, the conversion of the will. It is not so with the liturgy. The fact that the latter has no place in the Spiritual Exercises is proof of this.[1] The liturgy wishes to teach, but not by means of an artificial system of aim-conscious educational influences; it simply creates an entire spiritual world in which the soul can live according to the requirements of its nature. The difference resembles that which exists between a gymnasium, in which every detail of the apparatus and every exercise aims at a calculated effect, and the open woods and fields. In the first everything is consciously directed towards discipline and development, in the second life is lived with Nature, and internal growth takes place in her. The liturgy creates a universe brimming with fruitful spiritual life, and allows the soul to wander about in it at will and to develop itself there. The abundance of prayers, ideas, and actions, and the whole arrangement of the calendar are incomprehensible when they are measured by the objective standard of strict suitability for a purpose. The liturgy has no purpose, or, at least, it cannot be considered from the standpoint of purpose. It is not a means which is adapted to attain a certain end—it is an end in itself. This fact is important, because if we overlook it, we labour to find all kinds of didactic purposes in the liturgy which may certainly be stowed away somewhere, but are not actually evident.

When the liturgy is rightly regarded, it cannot be said to have a purpose, because it does not exist for the sake of humanity, but for the sake of God. In the liturgy man is no longer concerned with himself; his gaze is directed towards God. In it man is not so much intended to **edify** himself as to contemplate God's majesty. The liturgy means that the soul exists in God's presence, originates in Him, lives in a world of divine realities, truths, mysteries and symbols, and really lives its true, characteristic and fruitful life.[2] . . .

Have you ever noticed how gravely children draw up the rules of their games, on the form of the melody, the position of the hands, the meaning of this stick and that tree? It is for the sake of the silly people who may not grasp their meaning and who will persist in seeing the justification of an action or object only in its obvious purpose. Have you ever read of or even experienced the deadly earnestness with which the artist-vassal labours for art, his lord? Of his sufferings on the score of language? Or of what an overweening mistress form is? And all this for something that has no aim or purpose! No, art does not bother about aims. Does anyone honestly believe that the artist would take upon himself the thousand anxieties and feverish perplexities incident to creation if he intended to do nothing with his work but to teach the spectator a lesson, which he could just as well express in a couple of facile phrases, or one or two historical examples, or a few well-taken photographs? The only answer to this can be an emphatic negative. Being an artist means wrestling with the expression of the hidden life of man, avowedly in order that it may be given existence; nothing more. It is the image of the Divine creation, of which it is said that it has made things "ut sint." [that they might be]

The liturgy does the same thing. It too, with endless care, with all the seriousness of the child and the strict conscientiousness of the great artist, has toiled to express in a thousand forms the sacred, God-given life of the soul to no other purpose than that the soul may therein have its existence and live its life. The liturgy has laid down the serious rules of the sacred game which the soul plays before God. And, if we are desirous of touching bottom in this mystery, it is the Spirit of fire and of holy discipline "Who has knowledge of the world"[3]—the Holy Ghost—Who has ordained the game which the Eternal Wisdom plays before the Heavenly Father in the Church, Its kingdom of earth. And "Its delight" is in this way "to be with the children of men."

Only those who are not scandalized by this understand what the liturgy

edify From the Latin, "to build"; to instruct or improve.

means. From the very first every type of rationalism has turned against it. The practice of the liturgy means that by the help of grace, under the guidance of the Church, we grow into living works of art before God, with no other aim or purpose than that of living and existing in His sight; it means fulfilling God's word and "becoming as little children"; it means

> " *The practice of the liturgy means that by the help of grace, under the guidance of the Church, we grow into living works of art before God.* "

foregoing maturity with all its purposefulness, and confining oneself to play, as David did when he danced before the Ark. It may, of course, happen that those extremely clever people, who merely from being grown-up have lost all spiritual youth and spontaneity, will misunderstand this and jibe at it. David probably had to face the derision of Michal.

It is in this very aspect of the liturgy that its didactic aim is to be found, that of teaching the soul not to see purposes everywhere, not to be too conscious of the end it wishes to attain, not to be desirous of being over-clever and grown-up, but to understand simplicity in life. The soul must learn to abandon, at least in prayer, the restlessness of purposeful activity; it must learn to waste time for the sake of God, and to be prepared for the sacred game with sayings and thoughts and gestures, without always immediately asking "why?" and "wherefore?" It must learn not to be continually yearning to *do* something, to attack something, to accomplish something useful, but to play the divinely ordained game of the liturgy and in liberty and beauty and holy joy before God.

In the end, eternal life will be its fulfilment. Will the people who do not understand the liturgy be pleased to find that the heavenly consummation is an eternal song of

---

Michal

Michal was the daughter of King Saul and wife of David. She reprimanded David for dancing before the Ark of the Covenant (a chest containing the tablets of the Law, on which the Ten Commandments were written) as it was brought to Jerusalem and "exposing himself to the view of the slave girls" (2 Samuel 6:20). Guardini is saying that David was justified in dancing joyfully.

praise? Will they not rather associate themselves with those other industrious people who consider that such an eternity will be both boring and unprofitable?

Endnotes

1. The Benedictines give it one, but do so in an obviously different system of spiritual exercises to that conceived by St. Ignatius.
2. The fact that the liturgy moralises so little is consistent with this conception. In the liturgy the soul forms itself, not by means of deliberate teaching and the exercise of virtue, but by the fact that it exists in the light of eternal Truth, and is naturally and supernaturally robust.
3. Responsory at Terce, Pentecost.

For Reflection

1.　Do you agree with Guardini that the liturgy is "an end in itself"? Why or why not?

2.　How might you participate more in the "spiritual world" created by the liturgy?

3.　Discuss the liturgy as a "sacred game." What does that mean?

4.　Are you ready to commit to a less purposeful life? How?

26 Walk the Talk

Introduction

Kurt Vonnegut (1922–2007) was a popular American novelist, satirist, and social commentator during the 1960s and 1970s, when American society was undergoing dramatic change. The decade from 1965 to 1975 was among the most tumultuous in the country's history. Vonnegut wrote about the dehumanization of society and called into question technical and scientific "progress" that left people without a fixed moral or social center. He also railed against the superficiality of popular culture and materialism, which reduced human beings to consumers. Gone were the stable institutions that had provided identity and direction for hundreds of years. Whether or not one agreed with government policies or the teachings of the Church (often Vonnegut did not), at least one could count on these institutions being there. They provided boundaries within which one had a definite place and a more-or-less secure identity. Without them, exposed to rapid scientific and social change, people found it hard to discover what it meant to be human. For Christians, being

> **Luddite**
>
> This was the name given to a member of a popular social movement in nineteenth-century England that opposed changes in the textile industry as a result of the Industrial Revolution. Ned Ludd, for whom the Luddites were named, was a weaver in the late eighteenth century. The Luddites of the nineteenth century adopted him as their namesake. A fictionalized character called Captain Ludd (or King Ludd or General Ludd) was created and named after the original Ned Ludd, and this character became the imaginary leader of the Luddites.

human, fully human, is the only way of forming a relationship with the Risen Christ and his Church.

In the following essay, titled "I Have Been Called a Luddite," Vonnegut warns of the danger in society's fascination with machines, which "cheat you out of becoming." By this he means that instead of focusing on the latest version of, say, a mobile phone and whether it has 3G or 4G technology, we ought to be thinking about the latest version of ourselves and whether we have improved. Have we become more intelligent, wise, moral, compassionate persons? Or are we bunkered down in our virtual hiding places only to visit places vicariously or collect coupons to amass points for "free stuff"? In our pursuit of collecting things, even the language has become childish. Perhaps this is to remind us that it is all a game. Vonnegut knows that something else is going on, something more insidious. Virtual living, virtual learning, virtual being cheat us out of becoming real human beings, which is what God wants for us. (Recall the emphasis on true human dignity in the reading from *Gaudium et Spes* in chapter 19.) Vonnegut recognizes that there is a simple, human magic in observing and engaging with the people we find around us. He knows that we are living, breathing, dancing beings and that without community, without being in actual touch with real people—in good times and bad—we are less than human. What a sin it is for a human being to be less than human.

Vonnegut ends his essay with a line reminiscent of the previous chapter of this book, which has a reading from the liturgical theologian Romano Guardini. As you recall, Guardini exhorted us to waste time, to do nothing, to be present and enter into the divine encounter of the liturgy. Vonnegut asks us to do the same thing—to waste time, to talk to the guy in line about his foot, to get out and do something—which, he says, is what we're all on Earth for. So try it. You might like it.

Excerpt from "I Have Been Called a Luddite," from *A Man Without a Country*

By Kurt Vonnegut

I have been called a Luddite.

I welcome it.

Do you know what a Luddite is? A person who hates newfangled contraptions. Ned Ludd was a textile worker in England at around the start of the nineteenth century who busted up a lot of new contraptions— mechanical looms that were going to put him out of work, that were going to make it impossible for him with his particular skills to feed, clothe, and shelter his family. In 1813 the British government executed by hanging seventeen men for "machine breaking," as it was called, a capital crime.

Today we have contraptions like nuclear submarines armed with Poseidon missiles that have H-bombs in their warheads. And we have contraptions like computers that cheat you out of becoming. Bill Gates says, "Wait till you can see what your computer can become." But it's you who should be doing the becoming, not the damn fool computer. What you can become is the miracle you were born to be through the work that you do.

Progress has beat the heck out of me. It took away from me what a loom must have been to Ned Ludd two hundred years ago. I mean a type-writer. There is no longer such a thing anywhere. *Huckleberry Finn* was the first novel to be typewritten.

In the old days, not long ago, I used to type. And after I had about twenty pages, I would mark them up with a pencil, making corrections. Then I would call Carol Atkins, who was a typist. Can you imagine? She lived out in Woodstock, New York, which you know was where the famous sex and drugs event in the '60s got its name from (it actually took place in the nearby town of Bethel and anybody who says they remember being there wasn't there). So, I would call up Carol and say, "Hey Carol. How are you doing? How is your back? Got any bluebirds?" We would chit-chat back and forth—I love to talk to people.

She and her husband had been trying to attract bluebirds, and as you know if you have tried to attract bluebirds, you put the bluebird house only three feet off the ground, usually on a fence along a property line. Why there are any bluebirds left I don't know. They didn't have any luck and neither did I, out at my place in the country. Anyway, we chat away, and finally I say, "Hey, you know I got some pages. Are you still typing?" And she sure is. And I know it will be so neat, it will look like it was done by a computer. And I say, "I hope it doesn't get lost in the mail." And she says, "Nothing ever gets lost in the mail." And that in fact has been my experience. I never have lost anything. And so, she is a Ned Ludd now. Her typing is worthless.

Anyway, I take my pages, and I have this thing made out of steel, it's called a paper clip, and I put my pages together, being careful to number them, too, of course. So I go downstairs, to take off, and I pass my wife, the photo journalist Jill Krementz, who was bloody high tech then, and is even higher tech now. She calls out, "Where are you going?" Her favorite reading when she was a girl was Nancy Drew mysteries, you know, the girl detective. So she can't help but ask, "Where are you going?" And I say, "I am going out to get an envelope." And she says, "Well, you're not a poor man. Why don't you buy a thousand envelopes? They'll deliver them, and you can put them in a closet." And I say, "Hush."

So I go down the steps, and this is on 48th Street in New York City between Second Avenue and Third, and I go out to this newsstand across the street where they sell magazines and lottery tickets and stationery. And I know their stock very well, and so I get an envelope, a manila envelope.

It is as though whoever made that envelope knew what size of paper I'm using. I get in line because there are people buying lottery tickets, candy, and

What you can become is the miracle you were born to be through the work that you do.

that sort of thing. And I chat with them. I say, "Do you know anybody who ever won anything in the lottery?" And, "What happened to your foot?"

Finally I get up to the head of the line. The people who own this store are Hindus. The woman behind the counter has a jewel between her eyes. Now isn't that worth the trip? I ask her, "Have there been any big lottery winners lately?" Then I pay for the envelope. I take my manuscript and I put it inside. The envelope has two little metal prongs for going through a hole in the flap. For those of you who have never seen one, there are two ways of closing a manila envelope. I use both of them. First I lick the mucilage—it's kind of sexy. I put the little thin metal diddle through the hole—I never did know what they call them. Then I glue the flap down.

I go next to the postal convenience center down the block at the corner of 47th Street and Second Avenue. This is very close to the United Nations, so there are all these funny-looking people there from all over the world. I go in there and we are lined up again. I'm secretly in love with the woman behind the counter. She doesn't know it. My wife knows it. I am not about to do anything about it. She is so nice. All I have ever seen of her is from the waist up because she is always behind the counter. But every day she will do something with herself above her waist to cheer us up. Sometimes her hair will be all frizzy. Sometimes she will have ironed it flat. One day she was wearing black lipstick. This is all so exciting and so generous of her, just to cheer us all up, people from all over the world.

So I wait in line, and I say, "Hey what was that language you were talking? Was it Urdu?" I have nice chats. Sometimes not. There is also, "If you don't like it here, why don't you go back to your little tinhorn dictatorship where you came from?" One time I had my pocket picked in there and got to meet a cop and tell him about it. Anyway, finally I get up to the head of the line. I don't reveal to her that I love her. I keep poker-faced. She might as well be looking at a cantaloupe, there is so little information in my face, but my heart is beating. And I give her the envelope, and she weighs it, because I want to put the right number of stamps on it, and have her okay it. If she says that's the right number of stamps and cancels it, that's it. They can't send it back to me. I get the right stamps and I address the envelope to Carol in Woodstock.

Then I go outside and there is a mailbox. And I feed the pages to the giant blue bullfrog. And it says, "Ribbit."

And I go home. And I have had one hell of a good time.

Electronic communities build nothing. You wind up with nothing. We are dancing animals. How beautiful it is to get up and go out and do something. We are here on Earth to fart around. Don't let anybody tell you any different.

For Reflection

1. Do you think Vonnegut's assessment of machines and computers is fair? Why or why not?

2. Technology is supposed to make life easier and give us more time to pursue real things. Is this your experience?

3. How much time do you spend every day on technology (social media, cell phones, texting, etc.)? Do you think you spend too much time with technology? Does a dependence on technology cause problems in other areas of life?

4. What effect does technology have on the quality of your faith life? Explain.

27 "The Sunshine of Darkness"

Introduction

In summer 2007 a book was published that became a *New York Times* bestseller. It told a story of unrequited love and included heartache, intense longing, secret letters, travel to distant lands, and a deeply personal account of one woman's abandonment. It became an instant favorite of reviewers and literary critics for the opportunity it provided to look into the soul of someone they thought they knew. Most of the world had felt that way too, from the woman's coworkers to her family and friends.

Nearly everyone thought they knew Mother Teresa, the "Saint of Calcutta," who had founded a religious order dedicated to saving the lives of the poor, especially children, in the slums of Calcutta, in India. If anyone had faith as hard and enduring as steel, it was this diminutive woman in the familiar white sari with the blue stripe and sandals. She and her new order, the Sisters of Charity, had saved so many lives and helped so many people that she was awarded a Nobel Peace Prize in 1979. The world looked at her as a voice of simple faith, steadfast love, and unshakable belief in the dignity of human

---

Saint Thérèse of Lisieux

Saint Thérèse (1873–1897) was a French Carmelite nun known for her childlike piety and devotion to Jesus. She taught what she called her "little way" of meekness and humility in following Christ, trusting in God's grace. Even so, she experienced trials and sufferings similar to Mother Teresa's. Pope Saint John Paul II named Thérèse of Lisieux a Doctor of the Church, the youngest person and only the third woman to be so named. Saint Thérèse is Mother Teresa's patron saint.

---

life, from the unborn and disabled to the poorest of the poor. If anyone knew the power and love of God, it was she.

And yet, she felt that God's power and love did not extend to her. The book that was published was her spiritual biography, a collection of letters written to her spiritual director and religious superiors over a period of more than sixty years. In these letters, she wrote of intense darkness and pain. Although she appreciated the help and assurance she received from her spiritual directors, she often

> ### The Dark Night of the Soul
>
> This spiritual treatise is an autobiographical work written in the sixteenth century by Saint John of the Cross, Spanish Carmelite mystic and contemplative monk. It describes the inner journey of the soul on its way to meeting God. Along the way, the individual must go through stages. One stage is the dark night—in which the absence of God is most keenly felt. The work consists of a poem and treatise and has become a spiritual classic.

felt, after she had begun her work with the poor, that God was silent. Yet her faith sustained her even amidst her trials and questions. How could God abandon someone who had devoted her life to following Christ and doing his work on Earth: feeding the hungry, clothing the naked, welcoming the stranger, giving comfort to the sick and dying? She even asks, "What are You doing My God to one so small?"

Mother Teresa's pain is palpable. Yet, as you read this excerpt from her spiritual biography, think about whether we should give up if God does not answer us in a way we recognize—or even at all. Does that mean God does not exist? Some have argued that Mother Teresa's story provides direct support for atheists for whom belief in God is folly. One thing is clear, however: Mother Teresa agonized over the absence of God in her life, but she accepted that absence as her own "dark night of the soul." It may also be helpful to think of Mother Teresa's suffering as reflecting humanity today. Her doubt, hope, longing, and despair are what we experience every day of our lives as part of the human condition. Yet, like Mother Teresa, we cannot allow our feelings to keep us from doing what we know to be right and good.

Excerpt from *Mother Teresa: Come Be My Light: The Private Writings of the "Saint of Calcutta"*
Edited by Brian Kolodiejchuk

A few weeks after handing these revealing papers to her spiritual director, in her first general letter to her sisters, Mother Teresa exhorted her sisters to grow in the virtues to which she herself aspired.

> Be kind to each other.—I prefer you make mistakes in kindness—than that you work miracles in unkindness. Be kind in words.—See what the kindness of Our Lady brought to her, see how she spoke.—She could have easily told St. Joseph of the Angel's message (cf. Luke 1:28–37.)—yet she never uttered a word.—And then God Himself interfered. (Cf. Matthew 1:20–23.) She kept all these [things] in her heart. (Cf. Luke 2:19, 51.)—Would that we could keep all our words in her heart. So much suffering—so much misunderstanding, for what? Just for one word—one look—one quick action—and darkness fills the heart of your Sister. Ask Our Lady during this novena to fill your heart with sweetness.[1]

Refusing to allow her inner suffering to be an excuse for failing in charity, Mother Teresa was striving to have a ready smile, a kind word, a welcoming gesture for each one. She expected the same from her sisters.

The second virtue she insisted on was silence. To envelop in silence God's work within her soul, as Mary had at the Annunciation, was for Mother Teresa an expression of reverence and trust. Mary, who "kept all these things in her heart," (Cf. Luke 2:51) was her model and, as in Mary's case, she hoped that God would intervene in His own time and way.

Not only had Mother Teresa kept a sacred silence to conceal her inner sufferings, but she felt that God was doing the same. She believed that His showering so many graces on her work was His way of disguising *her* secret! "I am much better & will leave for Delhi on Friday—on 3/—ticket[2] with a nice place to sleep all the way up," she wrote to Father Picachy. "You see God spoils me exteriorly and so the eyes of the people are held."[3]

Afraid of Refusing God

While she continued guiding her sisters with strength and wisdom, she was seeking help from her spiritual father, remaining, however, willing to renounce even that support, despite the pain that might result:

> May I ask you to do just one thing for me.—Please put on paper all the things you tell me—so that I can read it over.— Write as I wrote—to Jesus—& you need not sign either. I think it will help me—but if you think He won't like it—don't do it. I know you pray for me.[4]

She appreciated greatly the assistance Father Picachy provided:

> I am grateful to you for all the kindness & help you give to my Sisters & me. My prayer though miserably dry & frozen is often offered for you & your work for souls. The conflict in my soul is increasing—what unspoken pain.—Pray for me— . . .[5]

Part of the reason for the conflict was the fear that the inner pain might condition her response to God, and that in a moment of weakness, without really wanting it, she might turn from her pledge never to refuse Him anything. She wrote to Father Picachy:

> Pray for me, Father—inside of me there is so much of suffering.—Pray for me that I may not refuse God in this hour—I don't want to do it, but I am afraid I may do it.[6]

Mother Teresa continued to carry out her apostolate with great interest and zeal, and while she did not get any consolation from it, she rejoiced in others' joy as she wrote to Father Picachy:

Thank God all went well yesterday, Sisters, children, the lepers, the sick and our poor families have all been so happy and contented this year. A real Christmas.—Yet within me—nothing but darkness, conflict, loneliness so terrible. I am perfectly happy to be like this to the end of life—.[7]

"He Has Cut Off One More Human Help"

In April 1960, Father Picachy was transferred from St. Xavier's College in Calcutta to Basanti,[8] so Mother Teresa was to lose him as her spiritual director. As she had recognized God urging her to open her heart to Father Picachy, so now she recognized Him challenging her to give up this important support. In her parting letter to her confessor, she admitted that Father Picachy's transfer was a real sacrifice. Nonetheless, she accepted it with graciousness, serenity, and gratitude for all his help.

> Dear Rev. Father,
> Some years back when you gave the retreat to the novices—& I made it with them Our Lord forced me to speak to you & open myself, and then as if to approve my sacrifice he made you our confessor.—I have opened my soul with all its trials & darkness—and the working of God as you say—to you. Each confession & writing or speaking to you has been a great sacrifice—only that I knew for certain that I could not refuse.—I spoke to you—and now I just want to thank you for all your kindness to me—and your patience—for you put up with all my trials—repeating myself each time—yet you never seemed tired of it all.
>
> Keep my soul with all its darkness & loneliness, its longing and the torturing pain close to the altar.—Pray for me—much & often—for now it seems He has cut off one more human help, and left me alone—to walk alone in darkness. Pray for me—that I may keep up the smile of giving without reserve—Pray that I may find courage to walk bravely and with a smile. Ask Jesus not to allow me to refuse Him anything however small—I [would] rather die.
>
> I beg one favour of you, please destroy everything that I have written to you.—I wrote all these because I had to—but now they are not necessary any longer. Please Father, destroy them.
>
> To ask you to come—I think that I will not do but if Jesus asks you to come—please come I will be grateful.

Thank you for all the good you have done to the Sisters—and the wonderful way you have guided them always with your eyes fixed on Jesus & our rules.

My prayer for you will be a daily one that you may become more and more like Jesus—and bring many souls to Him.

God bless you, Father.

Yours in Jesus.
M. Teresa M.C.[9]

"Sacrifices Are Only a Means to Prove Your Love"

Before leaving for his new mission, Father Picachy became ill; for that reason his departure was delayed. This gave Mother Teresa an opportunity to write once again.

Dear Rev. Father,

How happy you must be with the gift of St. Ignatius. Yet, Basanti will have many a sacrifice ready for you.—But for you—who love Jesus and souls—sacrifices are only a means to prove your love.

> " *With me the sunshine of darkness is bright. Pray for me.* "

You begin well your missionary life, by being first a patient. I do hope you are better—and they will soon find the means to make you well. In all the houses the Sisters are praying for you & I only keep "smiling" for you.—Your feast day[10] will be soon—the Sisters & I send you our best wishes & prayers & may St. Laurence* obtain for you the graces you ask for yourself.

With me the sunshine of darkness is bright. Pray for me.

If you are able—the Sisters would be glad if you come for the 13th. On that day we begin the novena for our Society—please join with us.—

l looked for a picture for your feast—and this is the only one I have here.—He has helped me much—he will do the same for you.—The words on the top—was my program for 1960. Cut them off.

Pray for the Sisters often—they are still very young—in spiritual

---

*Deacon of Rome in the third century, martyr.

life and otherwise.—Pray for me that I may help them to seek and find only Jesus.

I hope you will soon be better.

God be with you,
Yours in Jesus,
M. Teresa M.C.[11]

Not unlike Bishop Picachy, Mother Teresa too had "many a sacrifice ready" for her in the decades to come. She was fifty years old and was about to begin a new phase in spreading her mission of love that would take her on numerous journeys around the world. "Love is proved by deeds; the more they cost us, the greater the proof of our love." These trips would exact their price in time, fatigue and public speaking and serve as further proof of her love.[12]

Endnotes

1. Mother Teresa to the M.C. Sisters, September 20, 1959.
2. A ticket costing 3 rupees. Either she received a discount or someone made a donation.
3. Mother Teresa to Father Picachy, October 27, 1959.
4. Ibid.
5. Mother Teresa to Father Picachy, November 21, 1959.
6. Mother Teresa to Father Picachy, December 13, 1959.
7. Mother Teresa to Father Picachy, December 26, 1959.
8. A town about 55 miles south of Calcutta.
9. Mother Teresa to Father Picachy, April 4, 1960.
10. The feast of St. Lawrence, Father Picachy's name day, is celebrated on August 10.
11. Mother Teresa to Father Picachy, August 7, 1960.
12. Mother Teresa to Father Edward Le Joly, S.J., quoted in Edward Le Joly, S.J., *Mother Teresa of Calcutta: A Biography* (San Francisco, Cambridge, Hagerstown, New York, Philadelphia, London, Mexico City, Sao Paulo, Singapore, Sydney: Harper & Row, Publishers, 1983), p. 179.

For Reflection

1. How would you describe Mother Teresa's inner spiritual life? How does it compare to yours?

2. Mother Teresa uses words like "darkness & coldness & emptiness" and "sharp knives" to describe her loneliness. Have you ever had a similar sense of loneliness? Can you describe it?

3. Why does she call her darkness "sunshine"?

4. Have you been asked to help others when you didn't feel like it? How did your feelings and actions compare to Mother Teresa's feelings and actions?

28 Defending, Not Defaming

Introduction

This excerpt from Chaim Potok's novel *The Promise* exposes the quintessential issue in religious education and discipleship: how does the Church preserve the faith and pass on the teachings of revelation—what God has revealed through the Law, the prophets, the Gospels, and the traditions of the entire people of God—and make that faith come alive for a new generation of believers? This tension is at the heart of all religious traditions. Two things must be done and, ironically, done at the same time: hold fast to the core of faith and also inspire young people to make that faith their own, using their own symbols and idiomatic expressions. Those with the responsibility of handing on the Catholic faith (the Pope, bishops, pastors, parents, catechists, teachers) deal with this tension as part of their ministry. But this tension does not weaken the faith. Rather, wrestling with teachings and trying to make them one's own is the task of all adult Christians, helping them to develop a mature, healthy conscience.

The following excerpt portrays a scene in which the main character of Potok's novel, a young man named Reuven Malter, is sitting for a series of three oral exams in preparation for *smicha*, or ordination as an Orthodox Jewish rabbi. In his research for the exams, he has

> ### The Talmud
>
> The Talmud is a central text of Judaism that contains the Mishnah, the written equivalent of the oral tradition of the Torah (the first five books of the Bible, often called the Five Books of Moses) and the Gemara, a discussion of the Mishnah and related writings. There are two versions of the Talmud: the Jerusalem (or Palestinian) Talmud and the Babylonian Talmud. Of the two, the Babylonian Talmud is considered more complete.

discovered a text in the Talmud in support of a religious view that his teachers have rejected. He has already discussed the text with his father, a Talmud professor, about his interpretation ("emendation"), and so stands by that interpretation. At issue here is one's view of revealed truth, whether in writing or orally. Is the truth set once and for all in a fixed way so that it can be handed down to the people, or (as Reuven describes the Talmud) is it "fluid, alive, like a body of rushing water with many tributaries leading into it and from it"? Reuven insists on the latter and argues that he is not defaming the teaching of Orthodox Judaism as presented in the Talmud but rather is defending it, making it stronger through serious critical analysis and reflection. His examiners, **Rav** Kalman in particular, want to maintain the inerrancy of previous interpretations and the authority of the Talmud.

The author, Chaim Potok, was particularly qualified to open a window to the world of Orthodox Judaism, as he was raised in an Orthodox Jewish home and later became a rabbi in the Conservative Jewish movement, a less restrictive form of Judaism. As Potok describes the encounter of two opposing views on Talmudic studies, you may be reminded of similar discussions you may have had with your parents, teachers, or pastor about your own faith in Christ and his Church. As you read this excerpt, you might also reflect on the nature of education itself. Is knowledge a thing to be given or handed over, or a process whereby one sees things in a radically different way (we call this conversion), or both? If it is both, how do these two dimensions interact within you?

Excerpt from *The Promise*
By Chaim Potok

Rav Gershenson sat quietly, smiling. We waited in tense silence.

Rav Kalman returned with one of the huge volumes of the printed Jerusalem Talmud. He had it open to the **Mishnah**. He put it down on the desk and, standing over it, read quickly. The text was an exact duplicate of the one found in the Babylonian Talmud.

"**Nu**?" he said in angry triumph. "Where is the Mishnah different? How is it different? It is the same!"

"It's been corrected," I said.

He stared at me.

"That's the Vilna Edition. It was corrected according to the Bavli." "Bavli" is the Hebrew term for the Babylonian Talmud.

"Reuven," Rav Gershenson said softly. "Is the reading you speak of found in the old Venice Edition of the **Yerushalmi**?"

"Yes."

Rav Kalman straightened and stood stiffly behind the table, staring first at me, then at Rav Gershenson, then back at me. He closed the volume of the Talmud and went with it out of the room.

There was another tense silence.

The Dean looked at me, opened his mouth to say something, then changed his mind, and was quiet.

Rav Kalman returned. There was a look of bewilderment on his face. He said nothing about the Venice Edition of the Yerushalmi, which he had no doubt checked for the variant reading. He sat down and asked me to explain a passage in *Sanhedrin*, which was the tractate I had chosen to be examined on. I explained the passage. We went from one passage to another in *Sanhedrin*, and then we were in the Mishnah which lists ten differences between cases concerning property and capital cases,

Rav Hebrew for "master," equivalent to the Hebrew word at the root of *rabbi*, a religious teacher, which means "my master."

Mishnah The oral tradition of the Torah, or Oral Torah, written down in the Talmud.

Nu Yiddish word meaning, "So?" or "Well?"

Yerushalmi A Hebrew word referring to the Jerusalem (or Palestinian) Talmud.

Sanhedrin A tractate, or section of the law, concerning the Jewish courts of law, which outlines basic legal principles of traditional Jewish law.

Gemara, Gemora A commentary recording oral discussions of the Mishnah that took place in the Palestinian and Babylonian academies.

and I recited the Mishnah by heart and instead of going directly to the **Gemara** that followed the Mishnah, I jumped a few pages to where an **Amora** questioned the number of items listed in the Mishnah, claiming that he saw only nine differences. The Gemara resolved the difficulty, but unsatisfactorily as far as I was concerned.

"The second Amora did not have the exact same Mishnah as the first Amora," I said, and then was silent, waiting.

The Dean's face went from its normal pink to very red. Rav Kalman's face was pale above the starched white collar of his shirt. And Rav Gershenson looked at me narrowly.

"Where is the other Mishnah found?" he asked softly. "It is not in the Bavli and it is not in the Yerushalmi."

"No."

"Where is it found?"

"In a manuscript."

"A manuscript," Rav Gershenson echoed.

"You saw this manuscript?" Rav Kalman asked loudly.

"The manuscript appears in the Napoli Edition of the Mishnah," I said.

"The Napoli Edition of the Mishnah," Rav Kalman repeated, staring at me. His entire world of learning was being challenged. All the mental gymnastics to which he would have subjected that passage of Talmud had been turned into smoke by a variant reading found in a fifteenth-century edition of the Mishnah.

"Where did you see this edition of the Mishnah?" the Dean asked abruptly, his voice a little high-pitched.

"In the **Frankel Seminary Library**," I said.

He gaped at me. I heard a thin sigh escape from

Amora, Amoraim A renowned Jewish scholar. *Amoraim* is the plural.

Frankel Seminary Library The library of the Jewish Theological Seminary of America. Named for a progressive European rabbi, the seminary was founded under the philosophy that Judaism and its laws had always responded and should continue to respond to changing conditions of society.

between his lips. He sat back heavily in his chair and said nothing. But his face was now a deeper shade of red than before.

Rav Gershenson said, quietly, "You found this manuscript by yourself, Reuven?"

"Yes."

"You studied the Gemora and thought there might be a different Mishnah and you went and found it?"

"Yes."

He nodded heavily. He was no longer smiling. He did not mind emendations that were supported by internal evidence in the Talmud itself. But to appeal to a reading that was not found anywhere inside the Talmud—that was dangerous. That sort of method threatened the authority of the Talmud, for it meant

> 66 *I was defending the Talmud, not defaming it. I was trying to add to my understanding of it by going to the original sources of the many statements it contained.* 99

that the Talmud did not have all the sources at its disposal upon which laws could be based. He shook his head slowly.

Rav Kalman sat stiffly on his chair, his eyes very dark. He seemed not to know what to say or do.

I decided then to go all the way. I had planned to do this tomorrow, for I was working in stages—first emending a text on the basis of a reading found within the Babylonian Talmud, then clarifying a text on the basis of a reading found outside the Babylonian Talmud but within the Palestinian Talmud, and finally showing that texts existed which were not found in either Talmud but which nevertheless had been used by the **Amoraim** in their discussions. Now I would show them that there were contradictions even within the existing text of the Bavli, that the text as we have it could not be regarded as a unity, a coherent whole.

I started with an apology. It was not my intention, I said, to cause anyone unhappiness or pain by what I was doing. Nor was it my intention to defame the Talmud. I was defending the Talmud, not defaming it. I was trying to add to my understanding of it by going to the original sources of the many statements it contained. I understood that this method had dangerous implications, I said, but it was the only way I knew to study Talmud. I quoted from the works of Luria and Perlow and Pineles and Epstein in support of my position. . . . Then I cited two Talmudic discussions in the Gemara of the tractate **Ketubot**. They dealt with similar problems; but it was obvious that neither Gemara knew of the other: one based law A upon law B, and the other based law B upon law A. Yet both discussions used virtually identical words. How was it possible for two separate discussions to contain the same words? Only if the discussions originated from the same source, a third source, which originally had contained both discussions in itself—and I reconstructed that third source.

I was aware of the presumptuousness of my words, for they implied that I knew more than the Gemara had known. So I kept saying over and over again that I was not trying to be disrespectful to the Gemara but was only trying to better my understanding of it.

They sat there, staring at me in stonelike silence, not moving, not saying anything, just staring.

I was quiet. My hands were sweating and I could feel beads of sweat on my back. The silence lasted a very long time.

Rav Kalman sat on his chair, swaying slightly back and forth. He had closed his eyes. Rav Gershenson looked down at the table. The Dean stared at them, glanced at his wristwatch, then stared at them again.

Rav Kalman opened his eyes. "Malter," he said quietly. "You will teach Gemora this way to others?"

"Yes," I said.

He closed his eyes again.

Ketubot A tractate, or section of the law, in the Mishnah concerned with women and family life.

Tanach Includes the first five books of the Bible (the Pentateuch) and the remaining books of the Hebrew Bible.

smicha examination An examination required before ordination as a rabbi, certifying knowledge of Jewish law.

"You use this method on the Five Books of Moses too?" Rav Gershenson asked softly.

"No," I said.

"And on the rest of the **Tanach**? On the Prophets and the Writings?"

I did not answer. I was torn over that question and

did not yet have an answer to it. But I did not have to answer it. These were questions of theology and they had no place in a **smicha examination**, and they all knew it. So I remained silent.

Rav Kalman opened his eyes. "I have no more questions," he said.

The Dean looked at Rav Gershenson. "No more questions," Rav Gershenson echoed in agreement.

"We will meet again tomorrow," the Dean said.

"No," said Rav Kalman. "I have no more questions." He looked at me as he spoke. "It will not be necessary to meet tomorrow."

The Dean stared at him. Then he looked at Rav Gershenson.

Rav Gershenson shrugged. "A meeting tomorrow is unnecessary," he said, very quietly.

The Dean asked me to leave the room. I rose and very respectfully thanked them for listening to me and for giving me the examinations. Then I went to the door. As I opened the door, I looked over my shoulder and saw the three of them sitting fixedly at the table. I closed the door behind me and went home.

*

The smicha examinations marked the conclusion of my academic year and I no longer had to attend Talmud classes. I spent my time writing my Master's thesis. The decision as to whether or not a student had passed his examinations always came in the mail two or three days after the last examination. Four days passed and nothing came in the mail. . . .

For Reflection

1. What do you think of Reuven's explanation of his scholarship and of his examiners' response?

2. Reuven insists that he is not trying to be disrespectful, presumptuous, or confrontational. Do you believe him? Explain your answer.

3. What does Reuven mean when he says, "I understood that this method had dangerous implications"?

4. Have you ever been in a position similar to Reuven's examiners (suspicion of something new) or Reuven's (advocating new ways and meeting opposition)?

5. Do you think Reuven is accepted for ordination as a rabbi? Why or why not?

For Further Reading

Bonhoeffer, Dietrich. *The Cost of Discipleship*. New York: Macmillan, 1963.

Brockman, James R. *The Church Is All of You: Thoughts of Archbishop Oscar Romero*. Foreword by Henri Nouwen. Minneapolis: Winston, 1984.

Chesterton, G. K. *Orthodoxy*. New York: Dodd, Mead, 1950.

Colledge, Edmund, and Bernard McGinn. *Meister Eckhart: The Essential Sermons, Commentaries, Treatises, and Defense*. New York: Paulist Press, 1981.

Companion to the Catechism of the Catholic Church: A Compendium of Texts Referred to in the Catechism of the Catholic Church. San Francisco: St. Ignatius Press, 1994.

Dollen, Charles J., James K. McGowan, and James J. Megivern, eds. *The Catholic Tradition*. Vol. 1, *The Church*. New York: McGrath, 1979.

Eliot, T. S. *Collected Poems 1909–1962*. New York: Harcourt, 1991.

Ellsberg, Robert, ed. *Dorothy Day: Selected Writings: By Little and By Little*. Maryknoll, NY: Orbis, 1983.

Flannery, Austin, ed. "The Pastoral Constitution on the Church in the Modern World (*Gaudium et Spes*)." In *Vatican Council II: Constitutions, Decrees, Declarations*. Northport, NY: Costello, 2007.

Guardini, Romano. *The Spirit of the Liturgy*. New York: Benziger, 1931.

Gould, Stephen Jay. *Leonardo's Mountain of Clams and the Diet of Worms*. New York: Three Rivers Press, 1998.

International Committee on English in the Liturgy Corporation (ICEL). "Rite of Penance." In *The Rites of the Catholic Church*, vol. 1. Collegeville, MN: The Liturgical Press, 1990.

John Paul II. *Novo Millennio Ineunte* (Apostolic Letter at the Close of the Great Jubilee of the Year 2000). At *www.vatican.va/holy_father/john_paul_ii/apost_ letters/documents/hf_jp-ii_apl_20010106_novo-millennio-ineunte_en.html*.

Johnson, Elizabeth. *Friends of God and Prophets*. New York: Continuum, 1998.

Julian of Norwich. *Revelations of Divine Love*. Grace Warrack, ed. London: 1901.

Kolodiejchuk, Brian, ed. *Mother Teresa: Come Be My Light: The Private Writings* of the *"Saint of Calcutta."* New York: Doubleday, 2007.

Marthaler, Berard. *The Creed: The Apostolic Faith in Contemporary Theology.* Rev. ed. Mystic, CT: Twenty-third Publications, 1993.

Milavec, Aaron, ed. *The Didache: Text, Translation, Analysis, and Commentary.* Collegeville, MN: The Liturgical Press, 2003.

Mueller, J. J. *Theological Foundations: Concepts and Methods for Understanding Christian Faith.* Winona, MN: Saint Mary's Press, 2007.

Newman, John Henry. *Tracts for the Times: "Remarks on Certain Passages in the Thirty-Nine Articles."* At *anglicanhistory.org/tracts/tract90/section4.html.*

Paul VI. "Apostolic Constitution on the Sacrament of Confirmation." In *The Rites of the Catholic Church,* vol. 1. Collegeville, MN: The Liturgical Press, 1990.

Potok, Chaim. *The Promise.* New York: Random House, 1969.

Schreiter, Robert, ed. *The Schillebeeckx Reader.* New York: Crossroad, 1984.

Vatican Council II. *The Dogmatic Constitution on the Church (Lumen Gentium).* At *www.vatican.va/archive/hist_councils/ii_vatican_council/documents/vat-ii_const_ 19641121_lumen-gentium_en.html.*

Vonnegut, Kurt. *A Man Without a Country.* Edited by Daniel Simon. New York: Seven Stories, 2005.

Vorgrimler, Herbert. *Sacramental Theology.* Translated by Linda Maloney. Collegeville, MN: The Liturgical Press, 1992.

Weil, Simone. *Waiting for God.* Translated by Emma Craufurd, with an introduction by Leslie A. Fiedler. New York: Putnam, 1951; reprint, New York: Harper Colophon, 1973.

Acknowledgments

Scripture texts used in this work are taken from the *New American Bible, revised edition* © 2010, 1991, 1986, 1970 Confraternity of Christian Doctrine, Inc., Washington, D.C. All Rights Reserved. No part of this work may be reproduced or transmitted in any form or by any means, electronic or mechanical, including photocopying, recording, or by any information storage and retrieval system, without permission in writing from the copyright owner.

The quotations in this book labeled *Catechism* and *CCC* are from the English translation of the *Catechism of the Catholic Church* for use in the United States of America, second edition. Copyright © 1994 by the United States Catholic Conference, Inc.—Libreria Editrice Vaticana (LEV). English translation of the *Catechism of the Catholic Church: Modifications from the Editio Typica* copyright © 1997 by the United States Catholic Conference, Inc.—LEV.

The quotations on pages 15 and 16 and in reflection question 1 on page 20, the excerpt on pages 16–19, and the footnote on page 114 are from *Early Christian Writings: The Apostolic Fathers*, translated by Maxwell Staniforth (England: Penguin Books, 1968), pages 105, 104, 106, 105, 106, 104–107, and 95–96, respectively. Copyright © 1968 by Maxwell Staniforth. Used with permission of Penguin Books, Ltd.

The quotation on page 22 and the excerpt on pages 23–26 are from *Saint Augustine: The City of God*, Books XVII–XXII, translated by Gerald G. Walsh, and Daniel J. Honan (New York: Fathers of the Church, 1954), pages 172 and 170–174. Copyright © 1954 by Fathers of the Church. Used with permission of Catholic University of America Press.

The quotations on page 28 and the excerpt on pages 28–31 are from *St. Peter Damian: Selected Writings on the Spiritual Life*, translated by Patricia McNulty (New York: Harper Brothers, n.d.), pages 58, 57–59, and 62–63, respectively. Copyright © 1959 by Patricia McNulty.

The quotations on pages 32–33 and in reflection question 2 on page 36, and the excerpt on pages 33–36 are from *Waiting for God*, by Simone Weil, translated by Emma Craufurd (New York: Harper and Row, 1973), pages 113, 188, and 186–188, respectively. Translation copyright © 1951 by G. P. Putnam's Sons. Used with permission of G. P. Putnam's Sons, a division of Penguin Group (USA), Inc.

The quotations on pages 37 and 38 and in reflection question 3 on page 42, and the excerpt on pages 39–42 are from the English translation of "Apostolic Constitution on the Sacrament of Confirmation," from *Rite of Confirmation* (*Second Edition*), © 1975, International Committee on English in the Liturgy Corporation (ICEL), in *Rites of the Catholic Church*, volume one, prepared by the ICEL, a Joint Commission of Catholic Bishops' Conferences (Collegeville, MN: Liturgical Press, 1990), pages 474 and 472–477. Copyright © 1990, the Order of St. Benedict, Collegeville, MN. Used with permission of the ICEL.

The quotations on page 44 and in reflection questions 1 and 2 on page 49, and the excerpt on pages 46–48 are from *The Mysteries of Christianity*, by Matthias Joseph Scheeben, translated by Cyril Vollert (Chestnut Ridge, NY: The Crossroad Publishing Company, 2006), pages 8, 10, 11, and 9–13, respectively. Copyright © 2006, The Crossroad Publishing Company. Used with permission of the Crossroad Publishing Company, www.cpcbooks.com.

The quotations on page 57, in the sidebar on page 57, and in reflection question 3 on page 62, and the excerpt on pages 58–62 are from *Dogmatic Constitution on the Church* (*Lumen Gentium*, 1964), numbers 9, 48, 42, 42, 9, 6, 8, 42, 48–49, respectively, at *www.vatican.va/archive/hist_councils/ii_vatican_council/documents/ vat-ii_const_19641121_lumen-gentium_en.html*. Copyright © LEV. Used with permission of LEV.

The quotations on page 63 and in reflection question 3 on page 68, and the excerpt on pages 65–68 are from *House of Hospitality*, by Dorothy Day, in the Dorothy Day Library on the Web at *www.catholicworker.org/dorothyday/Reprint2. cfm?TextID=449*.

The quotations on pages 69–70 and in reflection questions 1, 3, and 4 on page 76, and the excerpt on pages 71–76 are from *Revelations of Divine Love*, by Julian of Norwich, edited by Grace Warrack (London: 1901).

The excerpt on pages 80–83 and the quotation in reflection question 2 on page 84 are from *The Three Greatest Prayers: Commentaries on the Our Father, the Hail Mary, and the Apostles' Creed*, by Saint Thomas Aquinas, translated by Laurence Shapcote (Westminster, MD: Newman Press, 1956), pages 76–80 and 77.

The quotation on page 86 is from *On Commitment to Ecumenism* (*Ut Unum Sint*, 1995), number 5, at *www.vatican.va/holy_father/john_paul_ii/encyclicals/ documents/hf_jp-ii_enc_25051995_ut-unum-sint_en.html*. Copyright © LEV.

The excerpts on pages 86–92 are from *The Creed: The Apostolic Faith in Contemporary Theology*, by Berard L. Marthaler (New London, CT: Twenty-Third Publications, 2007), pages 295–299. Copyright © 1987, 1993, 2007 Berard L. Marthaler. Used with permission of Twenty-Third Publications.

The quotations on pages 93 and 94 and in reflection questions 2 and 3 on page 98, and the excerpt on pages 94–98 are from the English translation of the *Rite of Penance* © 1974, ICEL, numbers 3, 3, 5, 2, 4, 3, and 1–5, respectively, in *Rites of the Catholic Church*, volume one, prepared by the ICEL, a Joint Commission of Catholic Bishops' Conferences (Collegeville, MN: Liturgical Press, 1990). Copyright © 1990, the Order of St. Benedict, Collegeville, MN. Used with permission of the ICEL.

The quotation on page 95 is from "Joint Declaration on the Doctrine of Justification," number 31, at *www.vatican.va/roman_curia/pontifical_councils/ chrstuni/documents/rc_pc_chrstuni_doc_31101999_cath-luth-joint-declaration_ en.html*. Copyright © LEV.

The quotation on page 100 is from *Apologia Pro Vita Sua*, by John Henry Newman (London: Longman, Green, 1964).

The excerpt on pages 101–105 and the quotation in reflection question 2 on page 105 are from *Tracts for the Times: Remarks on Certain Passages in the Thirty-Nine Articles*, by [John Henry Newman and William George Ward] (Oxford; London: J. H. Parker; Rivington, 184?), pages 17–20 and 19.

The poetry verses on page 107, the quotation on page 108 and in reflection questions 1 and 3 on page 114, and the excerpts on pages 108–114 are from *T. S. Eliot: Collected Poems, 1909–1962* (Orlando, FL: Houghton Mifflin Harcourt Publishing Company, 1963), pages 153, 157, 157, 160, 41–42, 153–155, 157–161, respectively. Copyright © 1948 by Faber and Faber; renewed 1976 by Esme Valerie Eliot. Used with permission of Houghton Mifflin Harcourt Publishing Company, and Faber and Faber Ltd. All rights reserved.

The quotations on page 116 and in the sidebar on page 116 are from *Evangelii Nuntiandi*, numbers 14 and 15, at *www.vatican.va/holy_father/paul_vi/ apost_exhortations/documents/hf_p-vi_exh_19751208_evangelii-nuntiandi_en.html*. Copyright © LEV.

The excerpt on pages 118–120 and the quotations in reflection questions 1 and 2 on page 120 are from *The Schillebeeckx Reader*, [by Edward Schillebeeckx], edited by Robert Schreiter (New York: Crossroad Publishing, 1984), pages 253–254 and 253. Copyright © 1984 by the Crossroad Publishing Company. Used with permission of the Edward Schillebeeckx Foundation, the Netherlands.

The quotations on pages 121 and 122 and in reflection questions 2 and 3, on page 125, and the excerpt on pages 122–125 are from *Orthodoxy*, by G. K. Chesterton, 1908.

The quotations on pages 126 and 127 and in reflection questions 2 and 3 on page 132, and the excerpt on pages 128–132 are from *Pastoral Constitution on the Church in the Modern World* (*Gaudium et Spes*, 1965), numbers 1, 26, 25, 26, and 24–28, respectively, in *Vatican Council II: Constitutions, Decrees, Declarations*, Austin Flannery, general editor (New York: Costello Publishing Company, 1996). Copyright © 1996 by Reverend Austin Flannery. Used with permission of Costello Publishing Company.

The quotations on pages 133 and 134 and the excerpt on pages 135–137 are from *Leonardo's Mountain of Clams and the Diet of Worms: Essays on Natural History*, by Stephen Jay Gould (New York: Harmony Books, 1998), pages 269, 276, and 281–283, respectively. Copyright © 1998 by Turbo, Inc. Used with permission of Harmony Books, a division of Random House.

The quotation from John Paul II on page 133 is from "Lessons of the Galileo Case," an address to the Pontifical Academy of Sciences, as quoted in *Origins*, volume 22, November 12, 1992.

The quotations on pages 139 and 140 and in reflection questions 1 and 4 on page 145, and the excerpt on pages 140–145 are from *Friends of God and Prophets: A Feminist Theological Reading of the Communion of Saints*, by Elizabeth A. Johnson (New York: Continuum Publishing Company, 1998), pages 231, 233, and 230–234, respectively. Copyright © 1998 by Elizabeth A. Johnson. Used with permission of Continuum International Publishing Group.

The excerpt on pages 147–151 is from *The Cost of Discipleship*, by Dietrich Bonhoeffer, translated from the German by R. H. Fuller, with revisions by Irmgard Booth (New York: Macmillan, 1963), pages 45–49. SCM Translation 1948, 1959 copyright © by SCM Press. All rights reserved. Reprinted with permission of Scribner, a division of Simon and Schuster, Inc, and Hymns Ancient and Modern Ltd.

The definition in the sidebar on page 149 is adapted from the *Oxford Dictionary of the Christian Church*, edited by F. L. Cross and E. A. Livingstone (Oxford / New York: Oxford University Press, 1997), page 55.

The quotations on page 155 and in reflection question 2 on page 158, and the excerpt on pages 156–158 are from *Meister Eckhart: The Essential Sermons, Commentaries, Treatises, and Defense*, translation by Edmund Colledge and Bernard McGinn (New York / Mahwah, NJ: Paulist Press, 1981), pages 202, 288, 105, 202, 202, and 201–203, respectively. Copyright © 1981 by the Missionary Society of St. Paul the Apostle in the State of New York. Used with permission of Paulist Press.

The quotations on pages 159 and 160 and in reflection question 4 on page 165, and the excerpt on pages 161–164 are from "Apostolic Letter *Novo Millennio Ineunte* of His Holiness Pope John Paul II," numbers 2, 31, 31, 40, 30–31, and 40–41, respectively, at *www.vatican.va/holy_father/john_paul_ii/apost_letters/ documents/hf_jp-ii_apl_20010106_novo-millennio-ineunte_en.html.* Copyright © LEV. Used with permission of LEV.

The quotations on pages 166 and 167 and in reflection questions 1, 2, and 3 on pages 171, and the excerpt on pages 167–171 are from *The Spirit of the Liturgy*, by Romano Guardini (Chestnut Ridge, NY: The Crossroad Publishing Company, 1998), pages 95, 71, 66, 66, 71, 65–67, and 70–72, respectively. Used with permission of the Crossroad Publishing Company, www.cpcbooks.com.

The quotation on page 173 and the excerpt on pages 174–177 are from "I Could Have Been Called a Luddite," in *A Man Without a Country*, by Kurt Vonnegut, edited by Daniel Simon (New York: Seven Stories Press, 2005), pages 56, 62, and 55–62, respectively. Copyright © 2005 by Kurt Vonnegut. Reprinted with permission of The Permissions Company, Inc., on behalf of Seven Stories Press, www.sevenstories.com

The quotation on page 179 and in reflection question 2 on page 184, and the excerpt on pages 180–184 are from *Mother Teresa: Come Be My Light: The Private Writings of the "Saint of Calcutta,"* edited by Brian Kolodiejchuk (New York: Doubleday, 2007), pages 187 and 196–201. Copyright © 2007 by the The Mother Teresa Center. The writings of Mother Teresa of Calcutta © 2012 by the Mother Teresa Center, exclusive licensee throughout the world of the Missionaries of Charity for the works of Mother Teresa. Used with permission of the Mother Teresa Center. Commentary by Brian Kolodiejchuk, M.C. Used by permission of Doubleday, a division of Random House, Inc.

The quotations on page 186 and in reflection question 3 on page 192, and the excerpt on pages 186–191 are from *The Promise,* by Chaim Potok (New York: Random House, 2005), pages 329, 334, and 332–336, respectively. Copyright © 1969, renewed 1997 by Chaim Potok. Used with permission of Alfred A. Knopf, a division of Random House.

To view copyright terms and conditions for Internet materials cited here, log on to the home pages for the referenced Web sites.

During this book's preparation, all citations, facts, figures, names, addresses, telephone numbers, Internet URLs, and other pieces of information cited within were verified for accuracy. The authors and Saint Mary's Press staff have made every attempt to reference current and valid sources, but we cannot guarantee the content of any source, and we are not responsible for any changes that may have occurred since our verification. If you find an error in, or have a question or concern about, any of the information or sources listed within, please contact Saint Mary's Press.

Endnotes Cited in Chapter 6, "More Closely Bound"

1. *Lumen Gentium*, 11, as quoted in "Apostolic Constitution on the Sacrament of Confirmation," Pope Paul VI, *Rite of Confirmation*, page 474.
2. Ibid.

Endnote Cited in Chapter 14, "Second Mark: The Church Is Holy"

1. *Katholischer Erwachsenen-Katechismus: Das Glaubensbekenntnis der Kirche* (Bonn: Deutschen Bischofskonferenz, 1985), 126.